LAST TO
LEAST

A NEW DIRECTION FOR WINNING IN WORK & LIFE

J. CASEY RYALS

TABLE OF CONTENTS

INTRODUCTION

As an insurance advisor and a small business owner, I have longed to realize the efficiency and productivity of the systems of the human body, which I witnessed first-hand during my years in medical school. Imagine a communication network like that of the central nervous system, with automated responses to pain that change the position of the hand immediately when a hot surface has been touched. That kind of streamlined efficiency is not often seen outside of nature.

If our systems of supply and demand and delivery and feedback were as smooth as those of the human body, the productivity we could achieve would be unimaginable. Political and economic systems could finally reach the dreams of our most creative humans because the rest of us could actually make them happen! If multiple bodies could learn to function as synchronous whole, the results would be astounding.

Childbirth is the bodily process closest to multiple people functioning as one—and it mesmerized me. Some parents report they are emotional, others stoic, but not me. I was utterly in awe when our first daughter was born. I was, first, astounded by the strength of my wife. Second, I was amazed by the rawness of the process. Sure, technology and medicine have come a long way, but the birth process is very similar to the way it was experienced thousands of years ago. Third, I was enthralled that two cells came together, then divided and repeated that process until I was staring into the eyes of Livie Cate Ryals, my first daughter! When Aliza Case and Anna Brooks came along, I was equally in awe of the process. Legs, arms, nerves—each cell seems to know where to go at the exact moment in the process until all the complex systems fall into place, and a body is formed that is equipped to sustain life for the next 80 years or so.

In the process of childbirth, I am impressed by a particular type of feedback system. When a baby grows large enough to put pressure on the cervix, his mother's body secretes a hormone called oxytocin. Oxytocin causes contractions, which puts more pressure on the cervix, which causes more oxytocin to be released, and so on. We have actually learned to manipulate this feedback system. We manipulate the natural process of the body to try and be more efficient. As early as 1913, physicians used an extract (oxytocin) from the pituitary gland to try to induce labor. Soon after, around 1955, we created synthetic oxytocin, which is now used regularly to induce labor.

However, early on there were problems with the way we manipulated the oxytocin feedback system. Excessive doses of oxytocin led to uterine rupture. Too much oxytocin caused the "normal" contraction process to become overactive. There was plenty of energy created, but a lack of control or direction for that energy caused trauma. The manipulation of the feedback system was supposed to be life-producing, but it sadly caused harm instead. Manipulating oxytocin levels has only been happening for about 100 years, and there are still situations where mother and baby are put at risk. 100 years is relatively young in terms of human history, so there is certainly more to learn about inserting ourselves into the natural process. We are still figuring out the best ways to improve the feedback system during childbirth.

We are all familiar with the feedback loops in work and business. Work hard, get more, so you can then work even harder to get even more (and more and more). The "American Dream" is only possible in a capitalist economy. In a feudal system or a system like communism, your hard work could never change your status. However, capitalism is also only a few centuries old. Merriam-Webster defines capitalism as "an economic system characterized by private or corporate ownership of capital goods, by investments that are determined by private decision, and by prices, production, and the distribution of goods that are determined mainly by competition in a free market."[1] While capitalism has obviously created the wealthiest nations in history, we are still learning about this amazing system and the way it can operate.

In 1976, Milton Friedman, a representative figure of American capitalism, was awarded a Nobel Prize in economics. He longed to see markets operate with the efficiency of our bodily systems. His devotion to and enthusiasm for capitalism and free markets were cultivated by the success of his parents as merchants. Friedman made the famous statement, "The only social responsibility of business is shareholder profit."[2] Of course, few of us agree with that sentiment any longer. I would say even Friedman did not totally agree with it because he qualified the statement by adding, "As long as they stay within the rules of the game."

Of course, most people mean "legal" when they say, "within the rules." Others would add certain ethical and social standards to their notions of legality. There were already rules against monopolies when Friedman made that statement, so we knew there had to be some government interjections in the business process. We are still trying to determine when and to what degree these interjections are appropriate on a macro level.

In a purely capitalist environment, we would never have

government interjections at all. Private business owners would have no laws to govern practices. The only penalty for poor business practices would theoretically be the loss of customers. We now know that a purely free market is only free for some, so most wealthy nations have adopted a mixed economic system. How much or how little government should be involved in the market is constantly debated. We may not agree on how much regulation is too much, but we can see how allowing the market to determine who wins and loses is efficient to create wealth.

Therefore, all across the world, those trying to gain market share or increase profits are attempting to create feedback loops that drive employees towards higher productivity. Whether trying to secure a place in the market for our business or secure a place in someone's business for ourselves, we are trying to maximize our potential and remain healthy and happy. Productivity, in simple economic terms, is how efficiently we change inputs, like effort or time, into a level of outputs like money or awareness. Productivity is doing work. How do we take the effort, human capital, money, and equity we have currently and use them to achieve our desired outcomes? Because capitalism and mixed capitalism are still fairly new in terms of world history, we have reason to believe the process is still being refined. I see one area that needs work immediately! I think we have we become so fascinated with the feedback loop (time, effort, resources are rewarded by monetary profit) that we have missed the entire purpose of work.

This is going to be difficult to follow because many of us are so ingrained with the work equals profit mindset. When we hear a challenge to our thinking, we have a hard time accepting it because we just try to fit the challenge into the same model we are used to.

Work can be about something besides my profits and incentives.

Actually, it must be about something BEFORE the feedback loop of profit and incentives.

If a physician began to measure her effectiveness as a practitioner based on the contractions she could create with oxytocin and the oxytocin she could generate from those respective contractions, we would call her a sociopath. The baby being born alive is the point of any new technology. A child we can hold being born whole and healthy was always the ONLY goal of the childbirth feedback loop. If a doctor somehow became infatuated with the feedback loop itself, we would say that person was unfit to actually do the job of an obstetrician. Yet this is exactly what we are lured to believe when profit is the only purpose of work.

Imagine the most deranged physician continuing to check oxytocin levels and contractions, sometimes having babies born and sometimes having babies lost. She may "succeed" with some families. They may thank her for her hard work. Others will not understand why their baby did not live, but there is little concern from the practitioner. The physician may even wonder why some patients do not appreciate her contribution to the preciseness of the levels of oxytocin administered and her expert understanding of the feedback loop. If she was extremely convincing, she may get others so distracted that they purchase her brand-new training, "How to Manipulate the Oxytocin Feedback Loop."

I get it. I listen to self-proclaimed experts who have more money than me go on about how students of their methods can follow their system and achieve the "wealth" they achieved. Some have become a little wiser and have stopped talking about work altogether. They say we should all do what makes us happy. Happiness is the new profit.

Profit, happiness, and wealth are all outputs that we have constantly thrown in front of us when we try to do productive work. They are all a part of this feedback system like oxytocin and contractions. The experts are trying to determine how much is too much and are trying to create the equivalent of synthetic hormones and develop the best ways to administer them.

We have become obsessed with the feedback loop of capitalism. The point of work was NEVER to generate profit. The purpose of MY work was never ME at all!

Farmers can profit because people in the market believe they need food. Real estate investors can profit because people believe they need a place to live or a storefront to rent. Writers can profit only when someone believes their prose or poetry is more valuable than the money it costs to buy the work.

Profit is necessarily preceded by a need met.

Sometimes the market is not even aware of the need. We did not know we wanted a handheld device that we could talk, text, and tweet from when I graduated high school. When that device became available though, massive profits were generated ONLY because we believed that we needed the device more than the money it cost us to get it.

When we become obsessed with a part of the feedback loop that is necessary yet never the point of the system, are any more qualified to "practice" our work than the OB in the example?

I have been tempted to forget the true purpose of work and only focus on how that work will make me rich or happy. However, when I saw that true productivity was measured by the results that I bring to my neighbor (client, customer, member) AND my neighborhood (political and economic systems) I could not un-see it.

Do not get confused. A neighbor is not simply someone who lives nearby. When the phrase was first used, it meant someone who sleeps near me because my community or neighborhood was close to where I slept. Now, our communities can be online and include people who still live in our communities, but their physical home may be anywhere around the world. For my purposes, a neighbor is someone whose needs my work is intended to meet. A neighborhood is simply the communities and groups of neighbors who are affected when those needs are met.

Profit is a true feedback loop that comes when I meet the needs of my neighbors and the neighborhood where my work takes place. Profit is massively important. It allows me to invest in equipment required to meet more needs than ever. However, profit was never the point of work.

I wonder if treating "profit" as if it is the end goal rather than just a natural part of the process is contributing to an epidemic. The numbers change from year to year, but globally, employees reported that 85% of them feel disengaged at work.[3] One study cited record high engagement at 34%.[4] That means that still 2 of every 3 were disengaged at work, yet the article seemed to be celebrating. Disengagement cuts production in half as reported by Jim Harter of *Gallup News*. That means that it takes two disengaged people to do the same work as one engaged person.

If we are going to treat this lack of production and engagement, we must learn to talk about work in terms besides the feedback loop of profits and incentives. If we do not, we will continue to walk away from work confused and hopeless. We will continue to seek motivation or assume we have not found our passion. We will lead others toward the false end goals of profit and incentives, confusing and frustrating our followers.

Let's learn to practice our profession like a skilled obstetrician. If she turned her attention to the life of the child, everything would become clear. All the technology or research or innovation would be directed toward the life-giving process of childbirth.

We can give life in any work we choose if we go from *Last to Least*.

PART 1

NEXT WISE MOVE

For the last decade, I have been assessing the risks of families and businesses and helping them see their options. I show clients their possible future outcomes and prepare them to lead themselves into possible futures. We look at the current state of each client's wealth and we decide together how much risk they would like to take for future reward and how much risk they would like to transfer, mitigate, or avoid. After countless moments with families and businesses having these meaningful conversations, I realized that risk management is very much like self-management.

You may or may not be familiar with the term self-management, but you know the concept. Every leadership book I ever read says you cannot learn to lead others until you first learn to lead yourself. While there are distinctions between leadership and management, for our purposes, leading yourself and managing yourself will be the same. Many of the principles I learned helping families and businesses manage their risks are the very same principles I use to manage myself.

Always, there are too many variables to consider at once.

The sad fact is that we cannot be certain about how today's decision will actually change tomorrow. We can run scenarios, but if decision number four is dependent on the outcomes of number two and three and we cannot even predict number two until we make number one, it can be confusing and overwhelming. Often, these scenarios can be paralyzing.

In these moments, I help my clients make the next wise move. There are always future developments that are uncertain. A 20-year plan is important, but sometimes we have to simply make the next wise move. Seeing and making the next wise move is an important part of a risk assessment and is essential for every self-manager.

There are some risk-takers who will leverage all they have to see great financial results. The facts are that few of these risk-takers actually see the massive returns hoped for. That is not an opinion. Big risks that come with big rewards are also, by definition, only going to happen for a few. For me to tell one of my clients, "I had a client last year who invested in product X and if you do the same, you will have his results," would be irresponsible. However, that is exactly what some irresponsible self-help gurus are telling us constantly about our work. They want us to buy their system with the promise that we will have the same results they had.

If I told my clients, "You have endless options! There is really no limit to what you can do today!" I would be lying if I did not assess each person's starting point. There is no way a family making the median income could afford permanent life insurance premiums that would equal their monthly income. You would call me a crook if I sold that. However, when it comes to career self-help, I constantly hear people say, "You can achieve all your 'goals' if you put your mind to it," without ever knowing what that person's goals are, the starting point of their education, aptitude, or socio-economic status.

You cannot be whatever you want to be. Even if someone from your neighborhood achieved all the goals you want to achieve, there is no guarantee that you will do the same if you follow the same "steps" they did. I can never guarantee someone's future based on the outcomes of someone else's past.

So, why do I write a book on how to work?

Because there are patterns, no doubt. There are "paths" to walk even if all outcomes are not predictable. We know this and that is why we are tempted to follow people who are shouting that we should go on their path because, "You will miss out if you don't."

I do not see many people being honest about the patterns and the lack of complete control over the outcomes. I do not see an honest system of how to manage myself without an accompanying obsession over the feedback loop of profit over the undebatable purpose of the work itself. I know how it feels to advise a business owner who heard if they "Just (fill in the blank)" then they will retire early, only to reveal the results they heard about are not guaranteed. I know what it is like to sit with a family who is paralyzed as they decide which insurance products are necessary because a salesman told them they were "crazy if they did not (fill in the blank)" and then they read on the internet that they were crazy if they did not do the opposite.

The risk and consulting industries need people who will be honest about the next wise move. Suggesting someone's next wise move requires courage and honesty. When assessing risks, most people know, "small risk, small rewards," so some courage and risk tolerance is necessary. However, when assessing possible future outcomes, we need more honesty. When life insurance planning with businesses who have met with another overpromising advisor, I always say with a laugh, "Tell me when you will die, and I will hook your family UP!" Any recommendation about risk planning with life insurance must come with accepting I do not know when I will die. I must accept some unknown variables and be honest about them. Making the next wise move demands courage, but it also demands honesty.

I also know all too well how frustrating a loud, obsessive "oxytocin-obsessed physician" can be, to continue our analogy. I know how frustrating it is to be constantly incentivized with profit or time off. It can make you question your own sanity. It can make us feel like we are simply using our neighbors to get what we ultimately want, or that we are missing the point of work entirely.

Sometimes we see a glimmer of light and engage in productive life-giving work for a season, but when a manager takes the credit for our production because they "motivated" us by screaming us through it, we are drained yet again.

If you manage others this way, you may become confused. When you constantly yell "go," hoping to motivate the troops, you may be left with no clue why your same efforts sometimes "work" and sometimes are dismal. It may be that you have forgotten "the baby in the room." You may be too busy motivating people to hit goals that are disconnected from the true purpose of your work. Disengaging when we have no true purpose is inevitable.

If any of us are going to be engaged and productive in our work, we first must learn to manage ourselves. When you ask people how they manage themselves, though, you may get a look of confusion. I did. I think that is why marketing guru Seth Godin said there are "fewer still" good books about self-management even though he also said, "there could hardly be a more important topic."[5] The confusion about self-management stems from people being unsure of what you are asking them. We have so closely associated success with and acquiring wealth that the two concepts have become permanently intertwined.

They may think you mean, "How do you get rich?" or, "How do you manage your time?" Time management is an important part of managing yourself that involves scheduling time to do the things that are important and productive. There are hundreds of systems out there for that. Time marches on in the same way no matter what we do with it. Learning self-management is crucial to making the best use of our time. Time-blocking itself will not move the needle at all, especially not in the right direction, but it will help us prioritize the next wise move.

They may think you mean, "How do you lead others?" because the statement, "You cannot lead others until you first learn to lead yourself," is in every leadership book, ever. They know there is a correlation between self-management and managing others but tweezing out the differences is as important as knowing the difference between the feedback loop and the purpose of the loop.

There are thousands of people, you maybe, who are excellent self-managers, but because of the lack of clarity around the subject and the blurred lined between profit and purpose, it is difficult to communicate what self-management actually is. So when I asked others and looked for help from some of the best and brightest in my own industry and others, I realized that even if someone was a great self-manager, they often did not know how to teach others that important skill. It was simply "the way they did things," or some oversimplified version of the way they motivated themselves through the day in a specific direction. Therefore, just like with my clients, I tried to provide an approach to self-management that can help you make the "next wise move."

When I first set out to codify my own system of self-management, I really did not have it all clear myself. And I will show you how I slid right back into the old system. After being named the agency of the year in Georgia, I started receiving phone calls from all across the state. I went from being an agent at one of the largest and most successful agencies in Georgia, to managing a county with only 2000 people in the most populated city. When the feedback loop is the focus in a volume sales organization, moving to a small town can be frightening.

However, not only was my agency the number-one ranked agency in Georgia overall, we were also number one on applications for products sold, competing with agents in every large city in Georgia, including Atlanta. The achievement that initiated the most calls was not my own. An agent at our office named Chip had been with the company for 15 years yet had been unproductive and unengaged for most of his career. When I first became his manager, he was ranked third from the bottom in all of Georgia. Just 12 months later, he was only third from the top! A remarkable swing!

After Chip underwent this amazing transformation, the phones were ringing, and our office was buzzing with visitors. From all over Georgia, managers sent their unproductive and unengaged employees to sit with me, wanting to see how we spent our day. Honestly, most were unimpressed.

I told them that the main skill that Chip learned was not closing or prospecting, but self-management. They were unconvinced, but it was partially because I even allowed myself to slide back into obsession with the feedback loop of profit and recognition.

I had started calling Chip "Sid Bream."

Sid Bream was the first baseman for the 1991 Braves. In 1990 the Atlanta Braves, our hometown team, were in last place in the National League. In just one year, they were in first place. I was in elementary school at the time, and I cannot forget the excitement I felt. The Braves had gone from worst to first! I called Chip "Sid Bream" to signify and celebrate Chip's massive move up the ladder.

When I saw confusion in the faces of the agents who paraded through our little office looking for the "magic bullet," I was frustrated with the situation, but I should have been frustrated with myself. I was making the same mistake as our sociopathic OB, focusing on the feedback loop rather than the true purpose of the work. I was trying to tell them how Chip learned to manage himself and how he became engaged and productive with the actual work he was doing, but then I was talking about his rise to "first" like the Braves.

I noticed that I was like a lot of others I have since run into. I knew how to manage myself, but I was having a hard time trying to teach others to manage themselves. I knew if I did not find a way to communicate self-management, I could never actually "develop" a leader. Sure, I could teach someone to influence others, but that is not the same thing as developing someone into a leader. If self-leadership is a prerequisite to leadership and I cannot teach it, then I am doomed to simply recruit others who have learned it. I will never become a leader factory, just a leader talent recruiter.

It has taken years of interviews, research, and introspection, but I have been able to codify a system that will give you the path to becoming a self-manager. If you are already a better self-manager than me, it will give you the tools necessary to recreate yourself, rather than just hoping people figure out how to lead themselves. I was teaching Chip this system because we spent every day together, but I wanted to be able to give it those other agents who were just passing through.

I told Chip I was sorry I had called him Sid Bream. I really was sorry. We laughed about it, but we both knew we had done something that was entirely counterintuitive to an economic system so infatuated with the feedback loop over the purpose of work itself. We decided he had not gone from worst to first at all. He had gone from *Last to Least*!

IF THERE IS A PATH, THERE IS A GUIDE

If there is a pattern or a path, then there is a guide. The guide may not be standing in front of us, but the path, worn into existence from those who came before assures us that we are going the right direction. Self-managers know that ultimately, the path they choose is their responsibility. When I advise clients, I always let them know that I can provide them with the "schools of thought" behind planning for risk, but they have to be involved in these decisions. Wisdom is as much about accepting what is UNPREDICTABLE as it is about trying to manipulate what is PREDICTABLE. So, I will do the same for you. I will try to lay out the options and make them clear. Your first decision as a self-manager is going to be your own guide. You can pretend that you are not following a guide if you would like, but we all are.

In an unforgettable commencement speech at Kenyon College, David Foster Wallace made an amazing declaration about us all. Wallace explained that, when looking for the next wise move, we are all choosing a guide. The choice is a privilege, but it is also a burden of responsibility. According to Wallace,

> There is no such thing as not worshipping. Everybody worships. The only choice we get is what to worship....

If you worship money and things, if they are where you
tap real meaning in life, then you will never have enough,
never felt you have enough. It's the truth. Worship your
body and beauty and sexual allure, and you will always
feel ugly. And when time and age start showing, you will
die a million deaths before they finally grieve you. On one
level, we all know this stuff already. It's been codified as
myths, proverbs, clichés, epigrams, parables; the skeleton
of every great story. The whole trick is keeping the truth
up front in daily consciousness. Worship power, you will
end up feeling weak and afraid, and you will need ever
more power over others to numb you to your own fear.
Worship your intellect, being seen as smart, you will end
up feeling stupid, a fraud, always on the verge of being
found out.[6]

Wallace was speaking about all of life, not work specifically, but
the correlation is a short jump. He is saying we all live for something,
and we must choose that thing very carefully. The thing we choose
actually acts as our master. We get to choose, but immediately we are
also choosing a guide to walk behind, a center for our lives.

In the same way, we work for something, not just wander aimlessly.
We get to choose a guide to follow, but we are following something.
Are we following money? Are we being led by recognition? What
is the guiding purpose of our work? If money goes left, power stays
straight, and comfort goes right, who do you follow? Of course, if
we can follow all purposes simultaneously, we will be glad to do so.
However, there are inevitably times when the paths diverge, even if
only slightly. These are the times when it becomes clear who we are

following and the true guiding principle of our work.

Managing myself is simply choosing my guide. If you are not sure which guide you are following right now, then you are being led like the blind. Hear what Wallace said, "Everybody worships. The only choice we get is what to worship." For some, the first thing to do is simply identify what guide you are following and determine whether or not that guide is the best one.

We live in the northeast Georgia mountains. Hikers come from the entire southeast to see the view in my back yard. My wife loves to hike Mt. Yonah, about 10 miles away. The views are incredible, and the hike is energizing. The danger, however, is real. There have been hikers who have fallen and died in 2008, 2015, 2016, and this year that I know of. My wife would like to go with me on hikes, but she would rather go with our friend Shelly. Shelly's husband is Site Manager of a local park and familiar with the terrain. When Alli hikes Yonah with Shelly, she is confident. Alli with me and Alli with Shelly is the same Alli, however her guide changes the experience greatly. She makes her next steps, her next moves, with confidence because she trusts the guide in front of her. She knows her guide is trustworthy, so she cannot fail to reach the summit safely.

I am trying to provide a clear mental picture with the Wallace quote, but here is the straightforward version. Identifying the reason for work is essential. With unclear motivation and direction for that motivation, we will have tension between our different sets of beliefs and be paralyzed to take action. When we do act, it will be sporadic. Sure, we maybe "took a risk" or "did as we were told," but we were not managing ourselves. We were being managed by someone who does not know us as well as we know ourselves or by some unknown force because we had our eyes closed, groping in the dark. By managing ourselves with a clear purpose in mind, we can see clearly to make the next wise move.

I want to offer you a new guide for your choices at work. It's not me. You can make choices about you better that I will ever be able to.

Give someone a fish, they will eat for a day. Teach someone to fish, and they will eat for a lifetime. Lead someone today and they will make the next wise move. Teach someone to lead themselves, and they will learn to see the next wise move themselves ...and be able to teach others to do the same. They will be able to know which path leads to the summit and which one leads to loose gravel and unsure footing. I want to teach you to see and make your next wise move.

THE PATH MAY CONTAIN WEEDS

One of the most frustrating contributors to unproductive, unengaged work is false expectations. When leading others, we paint the picture of a path that we are going to show them, and they can simply stroll down the beaten path. That picture is often crushed before the first day is over. A friend who is a nurse was excited about her extra pay for working the night shift. After waking up at 3 PM confused about what day it was for the first month, she was not nearly as excited. I have met with founders who knew their product was going to be viral only to find out getting initial attention for even the greatest products takes cultivation and patience. The weeds of frustration and disappointment cause us to want to blow up or give up. Unrealistic expectations are partially responsible for the large percentage of disengaged workers mentioned earlier.

We have to stop thinking about how to avoid the "weeds" at

work. Work produces amazing fruit but dealing with the weeds is part of the job. At every level and every pay scale, there are weeds in our work. Sometimes, in order to get to the reward, we have to feed the weeds right along with the fruit.

I was talking with a farmer who was telling me about his wheat production. He said he plants in October, fertilizes in March, and then sprays for weeds in April. The spray kills the weeds but does not hurt the wheat. Why kill the weeds? Because the weeds steal nutrients and water from the soil and decrease the production of the wheat. Does the spray kill all the weeds? It does not. Does the fertilizer before spraying nourish the weeds along with the wheat? Is sure does. Spraying before fertilizer or to trying to pick each individual weed would greatly increase production costs. The farmer has to accept that the weeds are part of wheat growth and plan and manage himself accordingly.

We must do the same. We must learn to see frustrations and disappointments as a necessary part of our work. Sometimes we will actually be spending "nutrients" on weeds just like that farmer. Sales calls will be made that only produce fruitless conversations. Hires will be made that never add value to our organizations. Leaders we developed will leave for other jobs in other companies. All of these are frustrations and disappointments of work, but an excellent self-manager will not try to rid himself of all weeds, he will learn to steer himself through the weeds of work. When you choose a guiding purpose, it is there to lead you in the right direction even when the weeds are so tall, there seems to be no path at all. That purpose will steer you successfully through the weeds of work.

Remember, you get to choose your guide. Do not forget what David Foster Wallace taught us. We choose our guide and that guide becomes what we follow. Even though I am completely convinced about my guiding purpose for work, I do want to show you the alternatives. If you agree and choose the same guide I have chosen, there will still be times of uncertainty. Again, all work brings up weeds. Without exploring the other options, we may be tempted to turn back. Even when we are following the guide I recommend; weeds may begin to grow. If we consider our options, however, we can agree that all work brings up weeds and make a decision that will guide us even when frustration and disappointment seem to be choking our efforts. Let's look at the alternatives to *Last to Least* and see if they can produce the freedom and fulfillment they often promise. But before we do, I want to make you a deal.

THE THREE QUESTIONS AND A DEAL

Throughout this book, will explore the 3 questions we need to answer if we are going to steer ourselves effectively at work.

1. What is the guiding purpose of work?

2. Who achieves that purpose?

3. How do they do it?

The order matters as much as the questions, but I know we all want the answer to #3. "Just tell me what to do and I'll get it done," we think.

So I will make you a deal.

I will give you two things you can do today to make you more productive and engaged in your work, if you will keep reading after them. I want to start with #1 and #2, but because I know we all want #3, I will start there.

Question #3: How Do Productive People Steer Themselves at Work?

1. They Act Instead of Talk

Many of us have used the excuse, "Business is slow. I cannot be productive because it is dead around here." Acting instead of talking actually does away with this problem! When times are slow, we can catch up on all the things we could not get to before. We can take inventory, catch up on paperwork, make the calls we needed to make. Especially in business development or sales l when things are dead, we can set our course without interruption.

Teachers can use dead time to learn new skills. Health care professionals can use dead time to get to the paperwork that backs up. Small business owners can use the slow time to build the relationships they know they need but never have time start. Managers can use slow times to build relational equity. All these are tactics that fit under "act instead of talk". ALL productive individuals act instead of talk. They know that all their action will not be perfect, but they know a secret. I will tell you the secret at the end of the point.

We had been very quiet around our office and I heard someone say, "It's a ghost town around here." For an "experiment" I asked someone to choose a letter from A-Z. I called the first two people in my phone under that letter who did not already have business with me. The newest of my team members watched on while I called. I said, "Hey _____. How is COVID-19 affecting your business?" They told me how and after a few minutes I said, "I know everything is chaotic right now, so we just want to talk about something normal. I can't think of anything more normal than insurance. Who takes care of your home and auto insurance?"

Both individuals said something like "I have been thinking about changing. It's like you read my mind." When my team member heard this on the phone, his eyes widened in surprise. He thought it was the way I said it or some magic that happened, but it wasn't. The reason those calls produced new policy holders with our company is because acting is more productive than talking—always.

But you knew that already, right?

That is why we need question #1 and #2.

However, even before Question #1 and #2 there is a secret I promised you. What productive people also know that often the only way to learn is by doing. People learn more by doing than by reading, talking, or listening. I can say that I learned more about making sales calls b just doing it than by reading a blog post about it. So it would be in your best interest to stop reading and act.

2. Surprises Are Opportunities

Have you ever said, "I cannot be productive because I am so busy?" Perhaps you feel like you never have down time. One or another customer always needs attention, or someone always interrupts your planning. Have you ever done a time study? If not, I recommend starting today. Just before the streak of being the most productive agency in GA five years in a row, I did a time study. The *Last to Least* system of making your next wise move is partly a result of this time study. For two weeks I wrote down my actions every 15 minutes. If I was making sales calls, I wrote down their names. If I was playing guitar, taking a break, or even using the restroom during a 15 minute block, I wrote it all down.

I then went back with two highlighters, red and green. Every time I was doing productive work, I highlighted it in green. Every time I was not, I highlighted it in red. Then I asked myself a question.

How many reds can I turn to green?

It was during this time when I realized every surprise or interruption that happens in a day can be seen as an opportunity.

When you view surprises as opportunities, it does away with the problem of being too busy to do productive work. When things are busy, we can use each moment to fully serve the customer in front of us, making them aware of every opportunity where we can help them, or cross-selling other products when servicing a product they already own.

Teachers can use a student's interruption asking for clarification as a time to clarify expectations for the entire class. Health care professionals can turn interruptions of policy meetings into times to ensure efficiency in the future. Managers can see interruptions like COVID as an opportunity to prove their value as a leader. Every interruption that comes can be seen as an opportunity. Every industry has its moments of surprise interruptions.

Now we that we have overcome our own objections to lack of productivity by learning what to do when things are slow, and what to do when things are busy. This is not terribly new information. So why do we still lack productivity sometimes? Here is where we can say, "Well you don't know my situation. It's not so cut and dry." And I agree. There are always exceptions. But the exceptions are not the rule. Most of the time, the exception does not exist.

Often, the failure to do productive work is not because of external circumstances, but because of internal struggles. That is why we look for motivation, often in the form of incentives, to inspire us to move when we are not moving.

Here's the thing—the sensation of not moving is an illusion. We are always doing something, even when we think we are not. We are just doing the things we do not want to do. We do not need more motivation; we need a new direction.

Question #1 will help us find the new direction. *Last to Least* answers question #1 differently than any other system of self-leadership. There are many other systems that offer many other guides for our work. Before exploring the guide for the *Last to Least* system, we will want to consider the other options. Seeing the alternatives to *Last to Least* will help us make our next wise move.

Remember, when I advised my clients about Risk Management, I did not make their choices for them, I just helped them see the options and encouraged their next wise move. I believe *Last to Least* is your next wise move, but I want to be honest about the other systems with other guides for your work, so you can decide on your own.

If you decide *Last to Least* will be your approach, Question #2 will help us decide to take the new direction instead of doing the things we do not want to do.

PART 2

ALTERNATIVES TO
LAST TO LEAST

GUIDED BY WHAT MONEY CAN BUY

"There was a man who had two sons. And the younger of them said to his father, 'Father, give me the share of property that is coming to me.' And he divided his property between them. Not many days later, the younger son gathered all he had and took a journey into a far country, and there he squandered his property in reckless living.[7] This familiar tale is, of course, the parable of the Prodigal Son.

The younger son had access to his father's entire wealth when he was at home, but his father had a different set of values, so the son asked for the cash and set out to use it his way. I am not sure how he squandered his property, but the scene just before Mitya is arrested in *The Brothers Karamazov* comes to mind. Mitya and Grushenka wake up all the peasant women and ask them to come and play music as well as dance with them and for them. Dostoevsky paints a picture of "debauchery". The scene is sexually explicit, though Dostoevsky unfolds the story as tastefully as possible, but they are abusing the poor for entertainment as well as abusing alcohol.[8] The younger son was living it up.

I think we all have the same picture in our minds of a party that never stops. Two things jump out and I think you will agree they are common when we are trying to go from worst to first. The first thing we work for is to buy material possessions. We want stuff! Do you know anyone who has made possessions the center of their work? If we are tethered to possessions, we may give up pride or comfort to get them. I can tell if someone is "hitched" to possessions because I can see them being led by the overwhelming desire for the newest gadget or the fanciest ride. They may get themselves in massive amounts of debt to be able to have the biggest house they can afford. They may be asked by their family or friends to move toward comfort or time off, but they are always pulled back to the center by their drive to own things!

The "stuff" is actually changing for some. I read a CNBC article recently which tried to explain why millennials are spending more money on experiences than possessions. Our parents worked hard for a house, two cars, and a boat, but other generations are finding alternatives for those dollars. Although material possessions are still on the list for the next generation, the experiences we are able to buy has become the new fad. According to the article these desires for experience are causing demand for trendy startups like Uber and Airbnb. Experience is the "new black"[9].

Unforgettable experiences are yet another way we are using work to get what we really want. If I work hard for eight hours a day for 50 weeks, then I can live the other two weeks how I really want to live! Or maybe I can achieve this by starting a small company and being my own boss. I may never have the money the corporate ladder offers, but at least I will be free to hike the Appalachian Trail when I feel the urge.

I often see this with a desire to buy things or experiences for one's children, to give that child things the parent never had. It seems noble, right? We have a really big sports culture in my community. Families will work hard so they can afford to buy their children the newest and best sports equipment and to spend the weekends traveling to different fields or complexes. Sure, some of them claim the extra practice will help the children have an advantage and a shot to get that college scholarship and a chance to play in the big leagues. When I ask around, though, many of them admit they know their children will never see even the collegiate level of sports. They do say they just enjoy being at the field and the overall experience. Others working to buy experiences want to travel to the most remote part of the world or pull up a chair by the beach. They may even be willing to trade a balanced work and home life so they can afford to take one more trip this year.

All this is to say, we are not worried so much about what we are doing at work or how we are doing it, but that it provides the life we really want or at least the life we really want for our children. We are managing ourselves with money at the center.

GUIDED BY A SEARCH FOR GLORY

Let's return to the story of the Prodigal Son. The younger son saw his money as a trade for the material goods and experiences he really wanted. The second thing someone with a younger son mentality will do is try to use work to buy the kind of friends they wish they had. I will have to admit, this has been a recent temptation for me with my daughter. I love her so much, and I want to see her being accepted. Kindergarten is tough these days! So, I asked my wife if

I could send her with extra ice cream money every Friday and tell her to buy ice cream for a friend. I was not thinking about helping the school's economy or giving ice cream to someone who could not afford it. Don't judge me, you have your own problems. I wanted to use my work as a way to get the life for my child I really wanted for her. Specifically, to buy a friend.

I can imagine this new guy in the story coming into town ready to party and having the resources to make it happen. Imagine how many opportunists came around him during that time! The Eurythmics said it accurately in the 80s hit "Sweet Dreams" when Annie Lennox sang, "Some of them want to use you, some of them want to be used by you."[10]

When we are trying to go from worst to first, we are glory hogs. We will talk about the danger of working to live up to expectations, but this is a little different. The younger son was trying to go from worst to first—not by approval, but by popularity. You can definitely see examples of those trying to go from worst to first by just being known. They do not care if you agree with them or approve of them at all, but they care desperately that you know who they are. They are willing to spend countless dollars and tireless energy to become known. It does not matter at the time where the attention comes from, even if they have to buy it!

Let's say there's a new dentist in town. The dentist may lower his prices so he attracts more business, and he may have billboards on every corner. You may think that his main concern is getting large to make money, but if you talk to his CPA, you may see that all these tactics are depleting capital. He does not mind that he is making less profit, what drives him is the attraction of attention. Again, when we are looking at these themes, do not think I'm saying the goals of profit and renown cannot be achieved simultaneously. We know sometimes becoming popular will lead to more money and more comfort or even allow you to become more helpful to your neighbor. However, we have been discussing that your center purpose may threaten your other purposes.

What other practical problems are present when we view our work this way? I am in sales, so I am totally aware of the view of the slimy salesman. The reason we cringe at this image is because we do not want to be taken advantage of for another's gain. Isn't this exactly what we are doing when we work to make money and things? If I sell you something just so I can buy the home or car I want or send my family on an expensive trip, I am using you to get what I need. When I put my needs at the front of why I work and there comes a time when my best interest and the interest of my client collide, what do I do? I choose my wants over their needs.

There was a huge scandal in the Atlanta school system a few years ago. The administration was pressured to pass students to show the schools were doing a good job. When the tests were collected and the students did not pass, some of the teachers changed the answers to give the illusion of passing students, enabling the teachers to continue being paid to teach. They were not considering the impact of receiving a passing grade when the student had not mastered the material, but they were thinking of keeping their job so their own family would not suffer. The teachers and administrators may have been thinking of losing popularity with the parents of the failing students. Money for possessions and money for popularity is a chain which will keep us from moving toward the good of others and the good of our communities. This way of thinking is part of my past. I am hoping for the day when we can all agree—work is not just about getting the stuff we want or buying the friends we want.

GUIDED BY A DESIRE FOR RECOGNITION

The other brother in The Prodigal Son is interesting as well. His pride actually went a little deeper than that of this brother. Simple vanity says we want other people to like us, but deeper pride tells us we do not need anyone to approve us. We approve ourselves!

The younger son actually came to his senses. He came home to his father and asked for mercy. His father gave him mercy, but he also forgave his lost son, and also gave him grace. The father brought his younger son back into his house, allowed him to be called his son, and enjoy all the privileges! Listen to the older brother's response when this happened.

> Now his older son was in the field, and as he came and drew near to the house, he heard music and dancing. And he called one of the servants and asked what these things meant. And he said to him, "Your brother has come, and your father has killed the fattened calf, because he has received him back safe and sound." But he was angry and refused to go in. His father came out and entreated him, but he answered his father, "Look, these many years I have served you, and I never disobeyed your command, yet you never gave me a young goat, that I might celebrate with my friends. But when this son of yours came, who has devoured your property with prostitutes, you killed the fattened calf for him!" And he said to him, "Son, you are always with me, and all that is mine is yours. It was

fitting to celebrate and be glad, for this your brother was dead, and is alive; he was lost, and is found."[11]

The younger son wanted to go out and buy friends, but the older wanted the friends to come and acknowledge him! He wanted parties in his honor! He wanted a legacy for his good work. He thought that while his baby brother was out living the party life, he should be recognized as the elder statesman who had stayed with the family business and never brought shame to the father.

The truth is, the older son did not appreciate the gifts he had been given any more than his younger brother. The older brother's view of working to get money to do what he really wanted can look like living for parties in his honor. This may bring to mind those who give substantial amounts of money to charity with stipulations to have buildings or statues named after them, but it can happen on any scale. We can be greedy but still make sure a friend sees us drop a quarter in the bucket which has a hurting child's picture on it when we leave a restaurant. It can even be as small as being offended when someone does not give you the proper thanks you believe you deserve. If I feel this way, I did not do the deed for another person's sake, but ultimately, I was looking to go worst to first. They were simply the way to get a party in my honor.

Giving to charity is something near to my heart, but if I begin to give so I can have a party in my own honor, I have crossed over to the older son's view. Sometimes, the actions may even be the same, but with one gift your soul will flourish and with another it will shrink in on itself! If I work so I can get enough recognition to have a building named after me or simply so the newspaper sees my efforts and gives me publicity, then I am thinking like the older brother. Some people think the purpose of work is so they can make money to give away to a religious organization. There are even some who believe their work is nothing more than a place to go to do their true work of telling people about their faith.

Do not get me wrong, so many of these things are vital. I actually believe telling people about our faith position is highly important no matter where we are, work included. We interact with so many people through our work and talking to them about life's most challenging subjects is part of a life well lived. But when I see my work as a means to an end only, it distorts the true purpose and focus of the work itself. The distorted heart says we want to work and give away money to get a plaque. The same heart says I want to work and give away money to the church so God will treat me well. When we try to establish favor with God using our work and money, or live for parties in our own honor, we are still being self-centered!

Some care little about money at all but want the power and recognition. The thought of promotion drives people to work long hours and take advantage of the weaknesses of team members rather than supporting them. Someone tethered to power may confuse someone who is tethered to money, comfort, or their neighbor.

I have a friend who serves as a board member for a charity. The board was hiring a new President to lead the organization. During the interview, everyone loved the candidate, but after the board meeting ended, one of the members started talking to others and defaming the candidate. When my friend tried to understand the board member's actual problem with the candidate, there was nothing the other board member could point out. The truth is, even though everyone was in agreement, the other board member felt more powerful if he was the one who was influencing the others instead of coming to a group decision. The best candidate to serve the charity's neighbors was not being chosen because the center of the other board member's work was not the people at all, but his own power to make a decision. He was chained to his power and it caused him to fight irrationally for a less qualified candidate.

The goals that someone with the older brother's mentality have are different from those of the younger, but the heart is the same. The deterioration of the community is the same as well. Each of these types wants to use other people for his own gain. The older brother wanted the party, and the father's blessing for all his good work, but he failed to acknowledge the gifts he had been given! That is a part of the past and the dissatisfaction that comes when your focus on going from worst to first.

EXAMINING THE NEED FOR APPROVAL

We have decided that work should not just be about money and status—and I agree. We have decided to stop working for money only and have become more philosophical. Personal satisfaction is the new end goal. We want to feel valuable. Erik Erikson would describe this as our identity. Erikson, a Harvard educator, was the author who made identity crisis part of popular language.[12] Identity is the story I am telling about myself. It is the answer to "Who am I?". Identity is what makes us sigh in relief and say, "I am ok," or "I have a stamp of approval."

For instance, I am a husband, a father, a son, a brother, a friend, a colleague, an employee, an employer. I exist in public and in private. I am me when I am on my best and worst behavior. Identity is simply the common thread that makes me, "me" no matter which of these roles I am performing.

Can we look to work to give us the consistent framework that makes up me? What are we tethered to when we look to work to give us a consistent identity? We are taking an approval-centered approach to self-management when we look for work to give us an identity. In more traditional cultures, identity came from the approval of the family and our place in the system. I am who they say I am. Today, we are told to create our own identity. We are told to look for approval within ourselves. Sure, approval is an important part of self-esteem, but will it take us from worst to first as the center of our work? I believe you will know someone who has tried to manage themselves with approval at the center of work. They may work for money or to serve or to just relax, but if those purposes ever stop approval from coming to them, they will pull back to the center. Is managing ourselves with approval at the center of our work going to get us from worst to first?

Let's look at two different approaches to approval centered self-management and see if they can get us where we want to be?

GUIDED BY IDENTITY
(APPROVAL FROM OTHERS)

Pressure to perform is part of the working environment in which we all live. There are no doubt people are leaning on us to get our part of the job finished so the rest of the cogs in the wheel fit together and there is no stopping the production line. There is definitely a sense of satisfaction when we get a pat on the back or the email which says we have done a good job. Some of us begin to thrive under this kind of environment. We get a tremendous amount of self-worth from meeting the expectations of our manager or industry. We may be encouraged by managers to be fulfilled this way. It may go something like this, "Don't you want to be all that you can be?" or, "You would be so much happier if you would only reach this objective," or, "I can tell you from experience, when I hit this plateau, I was able to look myself in the mirror."

These come from a leader in your organization asking you to go from worst to first and motivating you with approval. "Won't it just feel good to hit that goal?" Most of the time, these statements are a picture of their own centers for work. They are often trying to help themselves, not you at all.

Opportunities to gain approval may come from a parent who wants you to live up to your family name or take over the family business. "We would be so proud if you became a doctor or minister," or whatever your family values. I have seen young farmers continue to plow the fields passed to them from their fathers even though there was barely enough profit to keep food on the table, simply because they knew it would make their father proud.

One of the most significant problems with centering yourself around approval is we can spend more time making things "look right" instead of having them be actually right. I was leading a small group discussion on vocation with a mixed group of professions. I asked the question, "What are some parts of your work that frustrate you?" A dean of a college department in the group began to explain the accreditation process for new programs the department adds. He explained how some of the pressure he felt was, "not to make the program helpful, but to prove that it was."

I am glad he continued to try to do the former even though the pressure was there. As David Foster Wallace helped us see, we are putting something at the center even though other aspects of work are important. If the dean had put the accreditation at the center of designing the program instead of the students he would be serving, then there would be a slightly different approach. Of course, accreditation is important for accountability, but the dangers of making this the end goal can distort the true reason the dean set out to create a new program; namely, to educate and prepare students to impact their communities.

The subtle difference can lead to corners being cut to become accredited and actually losing focus on the purpose of creating the course: the students' knowledge. I contacted this college dean after the meeting to ask him more about the accreditation issue. As we talked, I asked a question. "I guess what I really am trying to get at is, 'Do some people focus their attention on the accreditation to the detriment of the students?'" He almost interrupted me before I ended the sentence as if he could not wait to answer. "That happens ALL THE TIME!" he said, stressing the last three words for emphasis. Whether it is common core mathematics, making a sell that our boss asked for by a deadline, or accreditation for college courses, having the approval of our work, not the people we serve as the focal point is eroding the community. Ultimately, having these things at your center does not deliver the worst to first movement it promises.

There is a problem if we try to go from worst to first managing ourselves by approval of others if we succeed and there is a problem if we try and fail. What if we succeed? "Everybody hates a winner!" is a phrase that a 70-year-old co-worker, Randall, said to me as we laughed in his office. I had a great week and finished off the month ahead in the rankings, so I stopped by to let Randall tell me how impressed he was. He was always willing to pat me on the back and—since he was the senior member of our team—I always wanted his approval above others. That day he was not doing so great himself. He had a tough couple of weeks and could not seem to close any sales. He was working just as hard or harder than I was. He was not mean, but when I told him about my week, he was not ready to celebrate with me. "Everybody hates a winner," was his way of joking, but also telling me to go brag to someone else.

I was getting my value from my work, so it puffed me up when I did well. Look, also, what happened to my relationship with Randall. He normally was my greatest source of encouragement, but because I was wanting the approval from a job well done more than I wanted to serve those around me, it made him simultaneously question his own value and not want to encourage me at all.

As a husband to a wife who spends her life thinking about how to be a great mother to our children, I know even when other mothers celebrate themselves on social media, it can make her feel like the great things she is doing are not enough. Sometimes when we achieve our goals, we put ourselves on a pedestal from which we look down on those around us. We need to learn to manage ourselves, no matter if we are seeking approval or in a position to give approval to others.

Last to Least is the solution for both the braggart and the offended. C.S. Lewis said "Pride gets no pleasure out of having something, only out of having more of it than the next man... It is the comparison that makes you proud: the pleasure of being above the rest. Once the element of competition is gone, pride is gone."[13]

Other people feel repelled by our arrogance, and if they have not found *Last to Least*, they will also feel guilty for not having the success for themselves. We build a wall between ourselves and those around us by trying to get them to approve us. It is really a mess.

"Oh, come on," you say, "I'm just posting my day on Facebook, I am not trying to gain approval." How many times have you posted that time when you called a client three times and they did not respond? How many times have you tweeted about your lack of patience with your children? I have even seen some mothers who are making their personal goals to be overly honest on social media. Their new way to personal fulfillment is being "honest" about their struggles as a mother, so they post things like, "I have not washed clothes in a week." We are still posing in some way to seem MORE honest than the next person. We are trying to get a sense of identity from being approved and now we need everyone to recognize it! We are going worst to first and need someone outside ourselves to see it!

When we hear about famous, successful, people who end their lives, maybe we should consider the empty promises our culture told them to believe. We teach that you can find your identity (value) in what you achieve at work. When these elite performers accomplish a major achievement, the promise offered does not give them what they were looking for. You can pull name after name that said they still felt like a nobody even when the whole world knew their name. Surely there is something we work toward that will not leave us empty when we succeed.

We also have to be careful when motivating people this way. When I say, "I will be so proud of you if you hit this goal or that goal," and the person we are influencing actually hits the goal, we are now required to puff them up. While my employee still has a high view of me, my approval will give them the power to achieve my expectations. I will let them down, however. Not intentionally if I am a good manager or employer, but it will happen. If they are working for my approval and then they decide I have let them down or failed them, I have now disconnected their power source for continuing to do a good job.

Now, you may think, "Well I just won't let them down." You either have not been managing people long or you have an unrealistic sense of your team. We as managers can try to be perfect, but it just will not happen. The other option is to give our team a new and better power source that cannot be severed. *Last to Least* is that source.

But what if we set out to get approval by meeting expectations and we fail? What if we do not live up to the goals? If we do not live up, we begin to tell ourselves why we did not make the goal. We have to find the reason and pin the blame somewhere. We have to blame others or blame ourselves. If we decide to blame others, it deteriorates the fabric of our community. We are unwilling to trust others for fear of being abused, but others are unwilling to link arms with us for fear they, too, will be named if our venture goes south. If we, rather, turn the blame inward, we will still push others away. We say, "I am a failure. I went after success, and now I did not reach it and I do not deserve happiness because I did not achieve."

Look where the focus is again. This self-loathing is nothing more than the wolf of pride hiding in the sheep skin of humility. The self-hater is really having a conversation with himself. He says to himself, "I deserve more out of life than you can give me." He is still seeing himself as the kind of person that is due certain things from life that are being withheld from him, a blow to his very identity when he is getting approval from work.

When we put ourselves at the center of the universe, the outcome is less than desirable. I owe Tim Keller a great deal of thanks for helping me think through these problems with living up to expectations. In his short piece about humility, he gives an excellent example of how a person who is self-loathing is ultimately being prideful just like the one who is bragging. He says we are all puffed up or deflated. The one who is puffed up is obviously arrogant, but the one who is deflated was previously arrogant and is longing to be puffed up again. You can only be deflated if you have previously been inflated.[14]

Practically, relying on approval just does not keep us motivated to work. I have seen this on the most practical level with a former co-worker. She was ready to help and ready to meet the expectations of the clients, but inevitably she did not have the power to meet every single one. For example, clients might be angry about increasing rates which was out of her control. They may have been frustrated because I did not meet their expectations, but they were just taking it out on my team member. When they took out their anger on her and let her know she was not meeting their expectations, her tolerance went out the window. When people were nice to her, she was dripping with honey, but the moment they were harsh with her, she returned their anger.

We have all seen it. I am in a service industry, but when someone is harsh with us and they let us know they do not approve, we lack the power to continue to do the work well. We do not have a way to absorb the anger of the other person and then continue to serve them. She was working to be approved by our customers, not to simply meet their needs. The difference is miles apart. If you are working to meet the expectations and you fail, why keep trying? If we decide this person is unreasonable, we abdicate ourselves of further responsibility to them.

The clients who let my team member know she was not meeting

their expectations were trying to make her act on their behalf. Because she was trying to get her sense of fulfillment from meeting their expectations and was failing, she was crushed and blamed the person for being unreasonable. I hope you see trying to work for the approval of those around us is impossible.

Almost all counseling today is based on managing expectations. Counselors tell us not to worry about the expectations of others, but to worry only about what we personally want to achieve. I agree with popular psychology—there is a problem with trying to meet the expectations of others with our work, but there is also trouble when we get our sense of approval and identity from our own expectations.

GUIDED BY IDENTITY (APPROVAL FROM SELF)

At this point, we have realized what a mess is created when we try to work to live for the approval of others, so we are now setting our own expectations. "I don't care what you think," we say and attempt to find satisfaction and identity by worrying only what we think about ourselves. We make our own goals and targets and reject the expectations of others.

In an article for the *Huffington Post*, Gayle Hilgendorff asks, "Why do we work so hard?".[15] She begins the article saying we are born with love and comfort being our only concern until we were "taught" societal pressures from parents, teachers, etc. Hilgendorff says we work hard to live up to all the expectations. Her solution was simple: start working to live up to your own expectations instead of those of others and you will enjoy working hard.

What if we defined our true happiness as our ultimate

success?" she says. "Well, all of a sudden, working hard isn't so hard anymore. In fact, it's quite enjoyable! Working hard is good for you when you know what you are working for. Working hard reaps the greatest rewards when you are enhancing your life and the life of those around you. Years of chasing the life of a successful corporate executive was extremely hard work, until I started chasing my success as a life coach. Nothing is more exhausting than spending your days trying to help others find their best lives, but it's an exhaustion met with happiness at the end of my day.

Hilgendorff may not realize this, but she could have done the same thing as an executive. I wonder if the glimpse of joy she is getting is not because she changed careers, but she changed her focus. However, she would probably disagree with me. She says later in the article that, "When we understand what success really means for us as individuals, and not how we are influenced by others, we can let go of hard work being a life-defining attitude and embrace the freedom to work just as hard as we want to."

She is seeing work like most people do in our culture and like I did in my past. It is a way to feel valuable to ourselves and when you do not feel significant with your work you should change careers or work less—or less hard. I read that and it is perfectly in sync with the vocational heartbeat. I would have read this in college and nodded happily along to the piper's pipe, but I cannot "unsee" the flaw in my past. I was looking for my own approval and if I did not get the goal I set out for, I felt like I could just change the target and then I could achieve. If I am not hitting my sales goals, just tell myself the goals do not matter! If nobody is offering me a job, change the career path.

We can find ourselves unwilling to accept responsibility for our actions and ultimately blame others for not appreciating us. We will lose out on an amazing gift we have been given—the ability to change. When we flip our goals around every time we face difficulty, we will always remain the same person, we never grow or develop solid character, and we will never learn to persevere. We will be able to go worst to first, because we can redefine first at any time. This can last for a while, but then the sense of identity we are getting from hitting our self-made goals will crash down on us.

The truth is, we do not usually live up to our own expectations, and we are finally still unsatisfied even after rejecting the expectations of others. If we decide to set the goals and expectations of our work low enough that we always achieve them, we will also fail to achieve the satisfaction and identity we were looking for. Why? Because we will realize we are the kind of person who sets low goals. Working to get a sense of self-satisfaction by living up to the expectations of those around us as well as working to get satisfaction from self-created goals are ultimately not giving us what we are looking to accomplish. We stay on the lookout and think maybe a new job or a new boss or a new goal may be just what we need to make everything right. But we are in a maze with no exit. We need someone to bust through the wall and give us a completely new way. *Last to Least* can do that!

Shawn Achor is a research psychologist trained at Harvard University. The focus of his research? Happiness. He says:

> I found that most companies and schools follow a
> formula for success, which is this: If I work harder, I'll
> be more successful. And if I'm more successful, then I'll

be happier. That undergirds most of our parenting and managing styles, the way that we motivate our behavior. The problem is it's scientifically broken and backwards for two reasons. Every time your brain has a success, you just changed the goalpost of what success looked like. You got good grades, now you have to get better grades, you got into a good school and after you get into a better one, you got a good job, now you have to get a better job, you hit your sales target, we're going to change it. And if happiness is on the opposite side of success, your brain never gets there. We've pushed happiness over the cognitive horizon, as a society. And that's because we think we have to be successful, then we'll be happier.[16]

See what he is saying? If we tell ourselves we can be happy when we reach our goals, we are kidding ourselves. If we will manage ourselves by saying, "If I just hit this much revenue or this much notoriety, I will know I am someone. I will have the approval I need," we are setting ourselves, the neighbors we serve, and our co-workers up for failure. We need a way to work which keeps us from being crushed when we fail to get approval, but also keeps us from setting goals that are so low that we are unproductive or lazy. We may need to realize work is for a completely different purpose.

Work is amazing and necessary, but it does not have the power to give me a consistent identity. If I try to get my identity from work, I am expecting something it cannot provide. Managing myself according to worst to first is keeping me tethered to approval, but not rewarding me with the false promise of being first Don't you see, this is why you cannot just change a few things and go in the same direction? *Last to Least* requires the courage to overhaul our thinking.

PART 3

OTHER MISGUIDING VIEWPOINTS

When speaking of sovereignty and free will, Christians think of God's control versus our choice. Even many unchurched people believe there is some greater purpose or external force that drives what we do. Let's call it free will versus fate. In other words, is it all up to me, or are there other forces beyond my control that determine my future? I confess I believe all things are under the control of God. He is all powerful. I know there are philosophical problems I have to deal with along with that belief, but this is not the place for that debate. I will say explaining existence without God seems much more difficult than with Him, even as all powerful and all good. I also believe we have choices to make. Again, if I was speaking from a different worldview, I would say that I believe in fate, but we also have choices to make.

I addressed a similar concept from the beginning, but now I am dealing specifically with the spiritual. There are two spiritual errors we can make when trying to go worst to first. One, we can use God's sovereignty to cancel out our responsibility. Or to say it another way, we can think everything is predestined so our choices matter little, if at all. Two, we can use our responsibility to cancel out

God's sovereignty. Or said differently, we can think that nothing is left to fate, so there is a heavy responsibility with every choice I make. There is a spectrum of views as to how much and how little God is predetermining or how much is fated, but I want to think through the dangers of unbalanced spiritual responsibility. I also want to explore what I am chained to when I allow these views to control me instead of taking the reins and managing myself.

HELD BACK BY SKEPTICISM: IT'S ALL UP TO ME

What could happen when I think it is all my responsibility to get work done and forget God is in control of His universe? This is the more common imbalance. If you did not believe in God at all, it would make sense to work this way. (Although some philosophers, such as Richard Taylor or Peter Lipton, who do not believe in God, still hold that all things are logically determined, and our will is not truly free.) You can get the feeling of this pressure to determine your own future by watching a TED talk by Larry Smith. He is a professor of economics from Waterloo in Canada, whose work focuses on why people will fail in their careers.[17] Smith prods us to pursue our passions and says the reason people fail is because they make excuses about why they cannot pursue passions. Smith encourages his audience to pursue passions rather than just interests because true passion is necessary for a great career. According to Smith,

> You must look for alternatives so that you find your destiny...And if you don't find the highest expression of your talent, if you settle for 'interesting,'...do you know what will happen at the end of your long life? Your...

tombstone will say, "Here lies a distinguished engineer, who invented Velcro." But what that tombstone should have said...was, "Here lies the last Nobel Laureate in Physics, who formulated the Grand Unified Field Theory."[17]

Smith is claiming the way to rise up and have a great career (as he defines it) is to make all the right choices. You have to pursue your passions and stop making excuses. He even ends his talk dramatically by saying you will fail "unless" and then just walks away. The dramatic pause works to motivate his audience to see that a great career is in our hands and we must act.

You hear the same talk from celebrities many times. "If I can do it, you can do it."

My wife and I were watching a recording of *Ryan and Kelly* one morning. Ryan Seacrest spoke about his humble beginnings and encouraged other dreamers to keep dreaming and they would eventually find the success he found. My wife was visibly frustrated. Countless celebrities make these statements to perpetuate the view that success all depends on your choices. Of course, celebrities can make those claims on the back side of success, but is it really true to say anyone can replicate the same outcome by making the same choices?

Michelle Alexander refutes this logic in her groundbreaking work, *The New Jim Crow*. She writes that the election of Barack Obama is an argument that some make to prove there is no racial caste system in the US and then refutes the logic completely. She is telling us that just because one person can make the climb, it is incorrect to assume someone else is able to do the same. "There is no inconsistency whatsoever between the election of Barack Obama to the highest office in land and the existence of a racial caste system," she writes.[18] Read that again or you may think I misspelled a word. There is no INconsistency. She is saying there is a black President AND a racial caste system.

You may not agree with Michelle Alexander, but you must see her point. Just because one individual has risen to power or prominence does not mean other individuals with similarities have the same path open to them. If she is correct, then the same applies to any vocation. I may not have the experience to disagree with actors like Seacrest, who have gone worst to first, but think through the promise he is making to aspiring actors.

According to Actor's Equity Employment Summary, only 40 percent of actors are working in a given season and only about 13 percent on a given week.[19] I would hate to be in a room and hear the sneers when some of them hear Ryan Seacrest say, "If you just make the right choices, you can make it too."

Of course, choices matter, but when we get unbalanced, thinking that it all depends on me, we forget we are powerless in some areas. The reason this is so important to remember is because at some point—when reality smacks us in the face—we will be unarmed with the fact that some things are out of our hands and we may crumble under the failure. We will think we made the wrong choices and hate ourselves instead of moving forward with resilience and confidence. There is probably an age range where you can continue to think it all depends on you. At a young age we can always say to ourselves, "Yes that was a failure, but I just have to keep moving and make the right choices, and I will eventually get from worst to first." At a certain point down the line, this "future pacifier" becomes a current sour lemon.

What may I have become chained to in my work that is steering my decision to place the burden of my success solely on my own choices? According to philosopher Alvin Plantigna, I have chosen to tether myself to skepticism or skepticism has chained itself to me. Alvin Plantigna gives an amazing assessment of someone who is skeptical about everything, even our origins and purpose. Among many other awards in the philosophy community, Plantigna was awarded the Templeton Prize. The prize in normally given at Buckingham Palace to someone who has made a significant contribution to affirming life's spiritual dimension.

Plantigna asks us to imagine we are on a foreign planet and found a radio transmitting information that was otherwise unknown. The radio may be sharing what John Kennedy had for breakfast on the day of his assassination. Without knowing the source of the information, he says, we would scarcely trust it was true.[20] He argues convincingly that with an agnostic view of origin, we must take an agnostic view of everything. See that? If we are unsure of the grand purpose of life, how can we be sure if simple tasks are helping us or hurting us from reaching that purpose? How can I be sure if I should be kind or ruthless? How can I be sure if I should be content or dissatisfied? How can I be sure if it is "good" to be stressed or to relax? If I am not sure about the purpose of the computer I am using to type, I cannot be sure about its practical uses either.

We see this in two ways in the workplace.

First, we cannot see all the practical ways to work if we have disconnected with work's purpose. There can be multiple purposes, but do not forget what Foster-Wallace said, we don't get to choose if we worship something, only what we worship or work for. If we know that money is important, meeting needs is important, and influence and providing are all important, yet remain skeptical about which is our guiding purpose, we will be held back from realizing our potential. We will have divided allegiance to each guide and ultimately make little progress toward actually achieving great things.

I meet people like this often. They cannot identify this skepticism, but they move from job to job or project to project, but always remain confused about why they are producing little. They may say they have "monkey brain." They cannot focus their energy and so they are a mile wide and an inch deep at best. They think they need new scenery, but they really need a new guide for work. They have traded any traditional guide and just made skepticism a guide itself. Everything can be deconstructed, so I never have to really choose what is valuable if I am guided by skepticism. This guide always steers me toward self-reliance because I have learned to poke holes in every established purpose and so I think I need to find the secret myself.

Second, skepticism about life definitely leads to skepticism in the direction of our work. When many of us have become skeptical about our origin, we have also become skeptical about even the most pragmatic daily habits. We have learned to be skeptical of every client and every vendor we encounter when carrying out our work. When we actively or passively tether our work to skepticism, we may think nothing we do really matters, and everyone has ulterior motives. We may find it hard to trust and easy to manipulate. We will definitely think if we are to get something done, be productive, "progress" or develop the newest technology, it is up to me to make it happen!

Imagine a Marine entrenched across enemy lines. If he is unsure that anyone knows where he is and unsure if anyone will come to his aide, he will make decisions very differently than if he is certain that backup is only minutes away. If skepticism about God or fate is steering you, it will cause you to believe that your choices are all that matter.

This broad skepticism is causing us to think that every achievement at work is going to come about only by our individual effort and there is nothing that is pre-determined or up to fate. Therefore, we put down our heads and trample anything or anyone in our path. If we succeed, we conclude that everyone else could have done the same if they just tried as hard as we did. We then repel everyone except those who think they can use us to achieve their own greatness. If we fail, we may conclude that we did not do enough, or we change our view to the next spiritual option: everything is determined. Succeed or fail, is skepticism at the center. Is the pressure of "it's all on me" really taking us from worst to first as promised?

HELD BACK BY ENTITLEMENT: EVERYTHING IS PREDETERMINED

On the other hand, when we begin to use the fact that everything is up to fate or up to God to abdicate us from responsibility, the results can be just as harmful. Doris Day's classic, "Que Sera, Sera" tells the circular story of the fated life. A child asks his parent if she will be beautiful or rich and the parent answers with the refrain, "Que sera, sera. Whatever will be, will be!" Then the child grows up to be married and asks her husband about their future together and hears the same answer. Then, finally, the child is singing to her own children later in life and passing on the same message of the power of fate, "Whatever will be, will be."[21]

The problem with an "everything is fated" mindset is very personal to me for reasons I will discuss I shortly. I want to help you stay away from this unproductive and confusing space. I started my career trying to stay on the top of the heap. I had one thing in mind: I wanted to manage my own agency. I loved where we lived, and my wife did as well. As weird as it sounds to some, I learned to love selling insurance. I got to live in a smaller town that I love, make more if I work harder and got to spend quality face-to -face time with a diverse group of people.

My manager knew how to motivate me because I constantly told him my goal was promotion. I was doing everything in my power to get there. I was acting as though everything depended on me. I had a scary suspicion God was not concerned with my success, so I was determined to work hard to get what I deserved. Then something very different happened. I realized my faith in God and in his son Jesus was the most important thing in this world to me. When that happened, my wife and I decided God was working in our lives, and He wanted us to become a part of a different community.

The following story may be unfamiliar if you are not a believer in God, but this backstory is important. My wife and I went back and forth about moving because it would stick us in the same place for a while, but we were confident God was communicating with us clearly that our path lay somewhere else, so we made the commitment. The same week we made the decision to stick to the new community, I got a call from work. Finally, after four years, the time had come for promotion. The position I'd been striving for was opening up because of a retirement. My district sales manager came to talk to me before the job opened up. He said, "I think this would be a good fit, and nobody has earned it more than you!" I was so excited! My income would triple overnight, and I would be recognized as a leader among my peers! But I had made the commitment to God already, so I could not apply for the position.

Looking back, it is so easy to see how God was setting the right direction, but at the time, I was just making the shift to trusting him fully. It was a difficult time for me—and my wife as well. I remember her asking me if I was crazy. "Who turns down that kind of promotion?" she asked. She was right, I felt a little crazy myself, but I was confident it was the thing God was calling us to do. That caused a massive shift in the way I started working. I wanted to please God with my work and give up anything he called me to pass up. Let me just go ahead of myself here and say I do not believe God calls us to give up things for the sake of giving up things, but He does sometimes call us to give up things for the sake of others. We will come back to that.

I was ready to sacrifice my selfishness, but I was still immature in the process. This is where I got imbalanced with my spiritual sense of responsibility. With my newfound deeper trust in the Lord, I began to allow His sovereignty to negate my responsibility. I would spend hours praying for the Lord to send clients to my office and almost no time calling clients. I could see this lack of personal ownership played out in many different careers. The business owner who prays for God to send business, but never advertises. The teacher who prays for her students to understand the material, but never realizes she is not communicating well. The stay-at-home mom who asks the Lord to help her connect with her children but will not put her phone down. The entrepreneur who "just accepts" the fact that most startups fail. The physician who prays for wisdom but gives little attention to continuing education. I was looking to the Lord, but I had failed to realize the great responsibility He had given me.

What is the tether holding me to the center when I take this view? I think you will agree—it is entitlement. I do not know if I would have believed I was entitled at the time, but I cannot unsee it now. I thought God owed me the blessing of clients and prosperity without lifting a finger. Please do not hear me say, "God helps those who help themselves." No, it is not that simplistic. When we see God mainly as a help to ourselves, then we begin to expect Him to become predictable according to our own whims. If there is a God, He cannot be exactly what I expect or I would be Him—and I can assure you I am not, as my wife would attest! We may not see that we are tethered to entitlement, but when we find ourselves expecting God, or the Universe, for that matter, to bring things our way, we may be held captive by our thoughts and actions without knowing it.

HELD BACK BY COGNITIVE DISSONANCE

I finally came to rest in the fact that there is tension between this "spiritual responsibility." As I said before, most people trying to offer a solution will try to explain how fate and choice harmonize. As a music lover, I know when there is dissonance, I cannot call it harmony. No matter what explanation I have heard, there is no perfect harmony between the two statements: "God is in complete control" and "I have free choice." So, I just accepted the tension and realized that accepting this tension is the only practical way to live. The tension, or cognitive dissonance, between the two ideas cannot be harmonized. However, treating both statements as true keeps us from both skepticism and from entitlement. If we can accept fate and choice as true simultaneously, even though they never harmonize, we will not be held back by the cognitive dissonance. We will steer ourselves in a new direction toward success instead of vacillating back and forth and spending valuable time trying to create harmony that is impossible.

I shared a room once at a conference with another agent who became a friend. We were talking about spiritual things, and he made a great point, "If God knows who is going to change and who is not, why even try to do better?" This is a very common response to the idea of predestination in a post-Christian American culture, but this attitude has filtered into the secular world. Whether you believe Christianity is actually true and relevant or not, millions of people you live and work around have been shaped by parents who believe this. The idea of a greater force directing everything that happens is left over in so many of our minds, but that we have not taken the time to think through fully. My friend may not have been able to fully explain why he thought everything was fated, but I could tell from his question he believed it was. I remembered a great account that Luke, a reporter at the time when the accounts in the Bible were written, told about Paul the apostle.

> When neither sun nor stars appeared for many days and the storm continued raging, we finally gave up all hope of being saved. After they had gone a long time without food, Paul stood up before them and said: "Men, you should have taken my advice not to sail from Crete; then you would have spared yourselves this damage and loss. But now I urge you to keep up your courage, because not

one of you will be lost; only the ship will be destroyed. Last night an angel of the God to whom I belong and whom I serve stood beside me and said, 'Do not be afraid, Paul. You must stand trial before Caesar; and God has graciously given you the lives of all who sail with you.'"[22]

Paul was confident that God had communicated with him that his shipmates would be saved. There was no doubt in Paul's mind that was exactly what would happen. A few verses later is where the confusion comes in.

In an attempt to escape from the ship, the sailors let the lifeboat down into the sea, pretending they were going to lower some anchors from the bow. Then Paul said to the centurion and the soldiers, "Unless these men stay with the ship, you cannot be saved." So, the soldiers cut the ropes that held the lifeboat and let it drift away.

There was no problem in Paul's mind saying God had made a promise to save everyone and then turning around later and saying if they get off the boat, they will not be saved. Many readers of this passage may be left asking, "Which is it? Will everyone be saved or if they get off the boat will they not be saved?" Holding both views in tension is the only way to balance spiritual responsibility. The cognitive dissonance did not hold back Paul when leading the people around him to safety. God would protect them without qualification, Paul was sure. If they got out, they would die; Paul was sure.

After struggling with the concept that God could be in control while still allowing free will, I finally came to understand that there was a bigger story playing out and everything was not solely up to me. At the same time, I realized my choices matter. Being disciplined matters. One of my favorite proverbs sums it up: "The horse is prepared for battle, but the victory is from the Lord."[23]

This is my past, and the background that allows me to share my insights with you. I hope I've made clear how some of the forces we allow to guide us toward success ultimately miss the point of work and do not fulfill the promises of taking you from worst to first. I did not have *Last to Least* to guide me, so when I realized I had to stop being completely self-interested, I did not know where to put my energy. That was the start of my confrontation. I was figuring this out slowly, but I could see the same confrontation coming years later with my co-worker Chip, mentioned a few pages back. Chip had different struggles, but we both had to come to a critical confrontation where we got honest about the jobs we were doing and the driving force that motivated us. The confrontation looks different for each person, but there are a few similarities for us all. For me, it took a while to navigate because I was in uncharted territory, but my struggle served as a helpful roadmap for Chip. That's why I was led to write this—to provide a clearly worn path towards success for those who may be lost. If you are still unclear about what exactly *Last to Least* is, that is ok. The eye-opening experience of the confrontation is what makes way for completely understanding *Last to Least*.

PART 4

THE CONFRONTATION

My wife and I love the TV series *This Is Us*. With limited time to watch TV shows, we often find ourselves choosing one show that seems to reflect a particular season in our lives. Because we have three small children, *This is Us* is our show as I am writing this book. The series unfolds the story of a family who is expecting triplets but loses one in childbirth. They adopt a baby, Randall, who was born and abandoned at the hospital the same day their twins were born. Viewers get the benefit of watching the siblings as adults along with flashbacks to childhood moments that shaped and molded the twins, Kevin and Kate, as well as Randall.

If you have never seen the show, Kate is obese and has struggled with her weight her entire life. Those who aspire to greatness can relate to the episode where Kate—after being afraid for years to pursue a singing career—demands an audition. She is given the audition, but, after she sings about five words, the producer stops the band and thanks her for her time. Kate reaches down deep, and I knew what was about to happen. In my years as an aspiring songwriter, I wanted to confront critics head-on, but was too afraid to say what was brewing in my mind. You start to think you have what it takes, but there is just some unstated reason you cannot get a break. Not so with Kate. She blurts out her thoughts. "I am not going to allow you to dismiss me because I am not thin like her."

Then the producer calls the thin girl to the mic and asks her to sing the same song Kate just sang. Kate is a good singer, but the thin girl is noticeably better. The producer responds honestly and bluntly, but not cruelly, tells Kate the girl had been demoted to a back-up singer because she was not good enough. He says something like, "I don't care if you are a 6 or a 26. It's not about your dress size. You're just not good enough."

I loved Kate's reaction. It was not melodramatic, but so well played. She was pleased the producer had been so blunt with her. She did not walk away thinking she was a great singer, but her weight was in the way. Rather, she walked away convinced she did not get the part because she was not good enough.

We are confrontation averse! I would make that last sentence 100 font size if it was appropriate. For some reason, we have decided public disagreement is not civil. The problem has become that the only people having the public disagreements are those who are so angry they are bursting when they do speak.

The confrontation has to happen if you go from *Last to Least*. There has to be a moment of clarity like Kate was given. At this point in my writing, I do not know what happens with Kate's story, but I know two amazing options. She can either take the criticism and realize she needs to hone her craft and become a better singer, or she can realize her gifts are elsewhere and leave the dream behind for an even better dream to which she is more suited.

Again, all people are not capable of all things because people are gifted with different skills, talents, and temperaments. An honest confrontation helps us look inside to see if we are really moving toward work's true purpose, or if we are just envying the strengths of others and want their same results for ourselves. If we are ever to abandon trying to use work to go from worst to first, we have to take an honest look at what we are expecting our jobs to do for us.

This is tough, especially to the degree we have bought into the worst to first mentality. For me the confrontation was slow, but it was the clearest when I was asked to join an initiative called "Move the Middle." Move the Middle was an initiative designed to encourage those in the middle of the rankings to step up to the next level.

As I said previously, my decision to abandon the concept of worst to first happened when I was offered the promotion I had been working so hard to attain. I did not, however, jump right into *Last to Least,* so I had a few years in limbo. Those few years were a time for soul searching, but due to my previous success, I was still known as a mover in the organization. However, after a couple years of my production being in the 70th percentile, my manager had some doubts that I could live up to my previously shown potential. His way of confronting me was asking me to join Move the Middle.

Although I never told anyone just how much I hated the title, I could not stand it! Mediocrity is one of my greatest fears, and the name "Move the Middle" just shouts it from the rooftops. I have always thought going for something and failing would be better than always playing it safe and being just another average guy with an average life. But here I am in "Move the MIDDLE"! It was like one of those, "We know you can do it, we see endless untapped potential," moments. Nobody said that, but it is exactly the message I heard loud and clear.

Kate's response stuck out to me so much because I was familiar with it. There was no demeaning, no yelling, no excuses. I just was not seen as a leader in my organization any longer. I was seen as someone in the middle.

I have to say, my soul was flourishing during this time. I had a poor view of work still, but I had really begun to realize my life was not going to be like it was in the past. I was going to live for more than just "more," having realized what a trap that was. Move the Middle let me know I was seeing myself differently than those around me. I saw a person with clarity, where there was actually inconsistency. I saw a leader in me where there was actually selfishness. I saw a leader, but I was still simply "working hard" or "giving it my all" without having a reproducible and methodical way of being successful. Many people have a position, but not many know how to take others where they cannot go on their own. I was seeing myself incorrectly, but there was something more profound I was missing. I had died to worst to first, but I realized I had still not found a new motivation to drive me. I had not found a new direction to steer myself.

Move the Middle did let me know I was not seen by my peers as going worst to first any longer, but it also let me know I was not willing to go back to worst to first even if it cost me my job. It made me ask myself, "If you are NOT going to do this, then what ARE you going to do?"

Would you have the courage to hear the confrontation the way Kate did and let it propel you forward, in a different direction if necessary? Or maybe you would have the courage to stay the course, even when it seems mundane or uninteresting? Or would you dismiss the confrontation and keep running your head into the same wall, never going around or over?

I remember the conversation well when my buddy Brent and I stayed late to bemoan my placement in Move the Middle. We had discussions like this since I had been at the company because he actually got me the job. We constantly made plans about what would shake out to get us where we wanted to be. I looked him in the eye and confessed, "I wouldn't promote me right now if I was the decision maker."

I meant it! I took a look back and thought about my former success, but I also realized there it had been nearly three years before. I told Brent honestly that if I was making the hiring decisions, I would want to choose someone who could teach others how to be consistent, and I had not figured that out yet. An honest look in the mirror is important. Unless I can realize my need for a new way to work, I will never look for it. Unless I see that the path from worst to first produced results that are insufficient, inadequate, and miserly, I will never be open to another approach to self-management.

Here's an analogy for you. Imagine a tribe on an island who has been surviving on meager rations because they have outgrown the resources of their small habitat. They have never known another home, so they hold on and try to make use of every last resource until they are forced to confess they will never flourish. They are not sure they will find anything as they set sail, but they know they will surely die if they stay. Sometimes you have to reach a breaking point before you are ready to make a change. It took a breaking point for me to notice it was not the career choice that was the problem, but my approach to managing myself. I did not even know there were other lands out there, so I kept trying to make things on the island give me what they never could. I kept trying to get what work could never offer until I finally had open eyes to my own insufficiency. I want to look into some of the confrontations I think are imperative to changing into the kind of people we would want to employ, work with, hire services, or buy from.

I admit that confrontation is a tricky slope to try to navigate. Dale Carnegie would hate this part but winning friends and influencing people is not the point of this section. This is not necessarily a method to managing people, but to become the person we want those around us to be. For that, I think we can take a little honest confrontation. Chip, at my first office, got the extra blunt version of this confrontation because we had to act quickly. Do you have the courage to hear the confrontation and allow it to mold you, or will you remain in the worst to first lane?

CONFRONTATION #1: YOU'RE NOT THAT GREAT

You are not as good as you once thought! I know. Your biggest fan would be so mad at me right now, but come on, we have to admit it! If you cannot admit it, you have to get out more. I will start with an example from my own life to soften the blow. I am a wannabe singer like Kate. I have always loved it. When I was leading a worship band at a church near Athens, GA, one of the band members thought my voice and songs were the "real deal." He told me this often. On a particular Sunday after we had played a song I had written he touted, "If you gave it one year and really gave it your all, you would make it. I guarantee it."

I believed him. I had already tried to get a few of my songs into the hands of people who could make things happen, but I had never tried to really "make it" myself. I started playing in some bars around the area, and our band had a great time. A year later we were not an inch closer to getting a record deal. It is ridiculously hard to get anyone to pay an unknown act to play, and they want the band to bring the crowd. My bandmate's belief in my talent had me thinking I would be on a fast track few musicians, even the great ones, ever enjoy. Then we went to Eddie's Attic in Atlanta to put ourselves in a competition for act of the night. I watched as a guy who sang like Marc Broussard, played like Dave Matthews, and even had a kick-drum and high hat that he played with his feet make me feel like the weakest excuse for a musician the world had ever seen.

Tim Keller tells a story about the same phenomenon. He is a minister in New York and says he has seen young people who were the best in their hometown come to New York to make it big, to get significance from their work. He says they get off the bus and see a street performer playing violin at the bus stop that is 100 times better than the new arrival. That is a crushing feeling. We have all experienced it. If you have not, it is coming soon.

Our talents are ours and there is no reason to be ashamed of being talented, but there are some amazing people out there with talents much greater than our own. They have honed their skills over years of dedication that make us feel tiny. Let's just all say it together, "You are not as good as you once thought!"

This year Forbes reported that there are 2,000 billionaires in the world.[24] You think you have a lot of money? Think about a billion dollars. That is one thousand million! It takes making $1,000,000/year for 1,000 years to acquire that kind of wealth. You think your money makes you great? It may help you feel good for a while, but at some point, you will meet someone with so much more, you will feel like me watching the talent at Eddie's Attic that night. You may put your head down and pass the person who made you feel "not that great," but soon you will meet someone else and someone else and to be blunt, only death will stop the cycle.

Maybe wealth is not your specialty and you are more concerned with your scientific aptitude. The Harvard Gazette reported this year Harvard scientists have applied 71.7 million pounds of pressure per square inch to a hydrogen molecule to form metallic hydrogen, something that has never existed on earth before this year.[25] You think you are smarter than everyone in your company? Join a professional organization and you will soon meet others that make you feel like a grade schooler once again. So, you are the expert? Do you think you have the capacity to create metallic hydrogen?

Not impressed by science? We are obsessed with fame and we judge it with retweets and likes. *Time* magazine reported that Ellen DeGeneres has the most popular tweet ever with over 3 million retweets.[26] If I get 200 likes, I feel like I am shutting down the web! How many people stop and listen when you speak? Really, if you had to get as many people as you could to an event in two weeks, how many would show up?

No? What about the extreme do-gooders? I went to the Catalyst conference earlier this year and I had a self-quake. After hearing some speak about the impact they are having in the world, all of my contribution seemed insignificant. Christine Cain talked about A21, an organization she founded. A21 is at work in 11 countries across the globe fighting to abolish slavery everywhere, forever. Jeremy Courtney was there talking about Preemptive Love, an organization that is on the front lines in Iraq providing relief and job creation. He moved his entire family there to risk their lives for the Iraqi people.

These stories made me feel so average and so tiny. Have you ever felt this way? We cannot enjoy the fact that slaves are being rescued around the world or refugees are being served, because we are too busy worrying about how this information makes us look or feel in comparison. I want a way to work that allows me to enjoy the accomplishments of those around me without worrying about how it makes me look or feel. The truth is, we are still being self-centered when the achievements of others make us feel small. If they are first, that makes us worst, so we lose motivation. Worst to first is like the judge in the courtroom saying, "Show me why you are worthy of first," and we look at our own standards and the standards of the brightest around us, and we have to admit we are coming up short. Remember, though, I have been saying all along that we are going to completely throw out worst to first and find a new center. There is a better way.

Some people are not impressed with the great achievements of other people. They have literally suppressed what they know to be true about greatness and decided the only thing that impresses them is—them. If you are in that camp, please wake up! That is the deepest pride. At least looking for the approval of others is still like a child looking for approval from a father. There is still some humanity in searching for approval outside of yourself. When you only care about your own opinion of yourself, you literally shut off the rest of the world and lose your humanity. Open your eyes to the wonderful things being done and be amazed by what is being accomplished in the world.

"Why?" you ask. "You're just going to remind me that I am not as good as I thought." I like that question. At least you are starting to care a little. Stick with me. There is more to this tough work of confrontation, but we are going somewhere beautiful.

CONFRONTATION #2:
YOU'RE NOT THAT SMART

The next thing you realize is your work is not as groundbreaking as you thought. After reading this section, you will want to learn proven practices in your vocation before you try to announce a new way of doing things. Here is where all the money I spent in medical school is going to pay off.

There is an example from the medical field which will help illustrate this fact. One of the first things we learned in medical school was how to do a great health assessment—also called a history—and a physical exam. Targeted questions and a physical exam are the tools physicians have used for years to gather information used to diagnose diseases. With so many technological advances, there are now hundreds of diagnostic tests to help doctors in this process. The tests include something as common as throat swab and culture for strep throat or as invasive as cardiac catheterization, but before a test is administered, there is always a good physical exam and history.

When someone walks into the ER with chest pain, it would be irresponsible to immediately prep them for a cardiac catheterization. The patient may simply have indigestion. Hear me carefully. A physician may see a patient and immediately have a hunch the person is having a heart attack, and the physician may be absolutely correct. Let's assume the hunch is completely accurate and the patient is truly having a heart attack. However, if the physician immediately gave the patient a cardiac catheterization, that physician would still be seen as irresponsible even if the hunch was correct. The physician should have used an EKG first to determine if there was reason for further testing. I will reiterate for effect that the physician should have used the EKG first even if they are correct about the patient having a heart attack based on the patient walking in with chest pain.

Based on the symptoms there is a "gold standard" or "criterion standard" within the medical community about which tests to administer in each situation. That gold standard is an accepted standard established by the industry and adhered to by the practitioner.

Every industry and every vocation has a set of gold standards. There is a sales process that helps a client see the need they have for a good or service and encourages them to spend the money to remedy the need. There are standards of practice for attorneys passionate about truth, standards teachers follow to instruct students, and even best practices for lifting heavy packages. Some of these standards are required by law, and some are as loose as accepted forms of behavior modification for stay-at-home parents. The world did not begin with our generation, so there is so much wisdom we can learn when becoming familiar with these best practices. Before we try to change our industry with an earth-shattering and innovative service, we should learn the proven methods that have gone before.

Researching industry best practices is not an attempt to create rigid conformity. The world would be so dull if everyone was just like me! Creatives continue to bring forward ideas that cause us all to have better work situations and better lives. Rather, my hope is that we will come in as learners before we become teachers.

Estee Lauder created and sold cosmetics like no other businessperson ever, but she learned retail and sales in her father's and uncle's businesses before starting her own. Tolkien created Elvish languages in his alternate world, but he began with a working knowledge of grammar basics. Tolkien's friend CS Lewis said, "In

literature and art, no man who bothers about originality will ever be
original, whereas if you simply try to tell the truth (without caring
two pence how often it has been told before) you will, nine times out
of ten, become original without ever having noticed it."[13]

Working according to what has been proven will bring the
result of creativity more so than setting out to be creative without
regard to the wisdom of the past. There are much grander examples
than my own, but I want you to see how practical this step of the
confrontation really is. Everyone should research what has been done
before they came along, from a secretary who thinks there is a better
way to transfer calls to a bellman who thinks of a more efficient way
to get bags to the room or a plant operator who designs a better
assembly line. The confrontation does not work to suppress a new
(and possibly better) idea, but the best way to get those ideas into
the marketplace is to first learn the marketplace you are entering. It
can be for an insurance agent who thinks he has found a new way to
prospect.

That was me! After a few years of success, I started to plan a way
to set myself apart from my peers. I asked to lead a group of elite
agents who would put our sales manager at the top. He allowed me
to lead the group, and I put together a PowerPoint to show them. I
admit fully, my main focus was to lead this group and prove I could
in fact lead an office! My actions were directed at making me look
great. I could not just give them what they had always heard, so I told
the how I had been successful over the last few years. The problem
was, my plan stopped working about the same time I was sharing it
every two weeks with the group. Instead of reminding people of the
tried and true methods of prospecting, I told them what I had done
that had worked. The ideas I taught had actually worked for me. But,

to build a successful career instead of a successful year, you need a center for working and a system of self-management that is durable.

I will thankfully admit I have come up with a few good ideas that have served my clients and employees well, but it was long after I accepted and learned the gold standards of my industry. Early on, my motivation was wrong, and I was not as innovative as I thought. I have seen this attitude at every level of skill, power, and education! When we think we are going to reinvent the wheel (and especially when we are motivated by the power or fame it will give us) we are destined to fail!

We are not as different as we thought!

CONFRONTATION #3: YOU CAN'T DO IT ALONE

There are some who are in the .01 percent, and they—literally—have it going on. They are satisfied with their work, and they really are the smartest person they know. I still stand by the fact they need to get out and meet a few people, but what if they really are that talented or that special? There can only be 100 or so who fit in this category. No, let's say there were 1000's of these extra-talented, super-rich, famous, movers and shakers.

I cannot help but point out though, even the A-list people are still lacking in some area. They are still missing something objectively and subjectively. Objectively, they need others around them to make up for their deficiency. They need others to do things for them they do not have time to do themselves because of the hours they spend doing whatever it is they do.

For example, I have people in my life who support me by doing what I can't or won't do. I have a good friend who cuts my grass, because he wants to serve me. Of course, I pay him, but he sees his work as a way to give me time. I tell him thank you all the time. I remind him how great a service he is to my family. I get to spend valuable time with my wife and daughters on Saturdays because he chooses to serve me by cutting my grass. I am so grateful for Hal. He is an amazing drummer and Bible teacher as well as being a Marine who owns a CrossFit gym. To me, it is worth paying for someone else to perform certain services so I can free up that time for myself or my family. I trade time for money.

I am constantly reminded how I could never have the full life I have without my wife being willing to make sure our three beautiful girls are constantly cared for. I cannot imagine my life without them, and I could not imagine my life if my wife Alli did not choose to be a full-time mother.

We need others. Period.

Mortgage officers need appraisers. Physicians need nurses, and surgeons need the salesmen who understand how the prosthetic knee operates. Every successful industry is dependent on other industries. Every successful start-up is never the result of a single individual effort. When small businesses reach a point where the owner can no longer perform all the duties, either the business plateaus or the owner becomes dependent on others to do what she can no longer do alone. These are obvious statements, but it seems that we so easily forget this blatant reality when we are set on being "self-made." We forget these realities when we are managing ourselves with money or approval at the center, but can we ever really say we do not need someone else?

I attended a "Farm-City" breakfast on the day I was working

on this chapter. The purpose of the event was to celebrate the interdependence of the agricultural industry with people who work in the city. There were farmers having breakfast with senators and real estate agents, dentists and agritourists. When I stood up to speak, I said thank you for coming to this "beautiful event." I acknowledged it may seem like an overstatement to call a nice breakfast beautiful, but I stood by it strongly. When there is unity within diversity, the result is beautiful. We celebrated the many different vocations represented at the breakfast and how we were all working together to make sure our community flourished. It took ALL these different vocations and people for the community to flourish.

Those who think they are good enough alone are not seeing clearly. Those who seem good enough alone appear that way because you just cannot see where they are depending on others to hold them up.

The idea that I am the most important factor in my own work is almost "common sense" today, but when we really think through it, it's just not true. Do you think that could be why we have feelings of anxiety, worry, and disgust around our jobs? Could we have begun to expect work to give us something it could never provide?

Food is for our enjoyment as well as to sustain life. If we make enjoyment the central reason we eat, we will soon be overweight and unhealthy. It works the same way with the purpose that drives our work. Could the anxiety and frustration we feel at work be caused by acting as though our central purpose is something other than what it actually should be?

CONFRONTATION #4:
YOU HAVE SOMETHING TO OFFER (YES, YOU!)

What if you are the one saying, "I never thought my work was innovative at all, I just load a truck!" Great start, I am coming to you as well. You may even look at a billion-dollar company and think, "I only manage a multi-million-dollar organization."

I think the message of *Last to Least* has the same effect as a road project I have been driving past on the way to work for a few months. The workers are creating a new bridge directly beside an old one on my drive to work. There is a river that flows under the bridge and on each side of the river there is a steep cliff which goes up about 100 feet above the current road. On the north side of the cliff (opposite the river), there is a small valley that dips back down as low as the river itself. As the road crew improves the road, they will do two things. They will lower the cliff, and they will raise up the valley. When they accomplish this task, the community will thrive because the level ground will allow us all to make it safely to our destinations.

Some are going to the school across the river to teach, others are buying or selling various products, and others will use the bridge for delivering packages and materials. Before all this happens, though, they will have to finish raising the low spots and lowering the high spots.

Last to Least has the same effect! *Last to Least* can cause the proud to be lowered, but it can simultaneously raise the lowly to create a community that flourishes. We have spent energy confronting those of us who think too highly of ourselves, but the low spots need to be brought up as well. Do not make the mistake of thinking you are being selfless when you are too embarrassed or too timid to step out to make a difference with your work. The confrontation is tough, but the hard work goes for the disheartened as well. Do not be tricked by negative self-talk into thinking you are a victim of a harsh world and you could never amount to anything.

You may think, "There is no way there is a greater purpose for my work. I do not have the talent or the money or the position or connections." You are still thinking about going worst to first. I want to be careful here because I want to be sensitive to the feelings we have when we are deflated. Most self-help gurus tell you to look into the mirror and say, "I am important." That being said, I think there is a better way to help you see your importance. While we should not be puffed up with pride because we are irreplaceable, you also cannot continue to see yourself as a disposable piece of the puzzle. Every part of an organization, or the economy for that matter, is like a body working together. You too have a responsibility and a purpose.

An eye cannot say to an ear, "We do not need you." Also, an ear cannot say to an eye, "I am not important." That means two things. First, we cannot be so prideful as to think we can do alone what an entire organization is set up to accomplish. If we feel this way, we will try to do more than we are capable of, as well as expect more out of others than they are capable of. We will be full of solutions for every problem, but we will frustrate the people around us because our "solutions" only answer one piece of the puzzle at a time, never addressing the whole. Second, we cannot be too deflated to think we are not an important piece of the whole. If you think there is no need for someone like you, this is a lie that needs to be combated. Before we talk about how to replace those thoughts, let's make sure we know where they are coming from.

If we think we are the most innovative and different, we may try to tell others around us how they should change to fit our mold before we ever know the proven patterns. On the other hand, if we shrink into a corner because we feel like we could never make a great impact because of our insufficiency, it's still a matter of selfish pride because the focus is on YOU!

The focus was the same for the younger brother and the older brother in the parable of The Prodigal Son. The focus was the same when I started a group that would make me look good to my managers. The focus was the same when Chip told me he was a good agent but was only doing half his job. The focus was also the same when my wife told me she would never be a great parent or when an employee told me he was not born with the "it" factor I had. The focus was self! The common theme in the worst to first mentality is who is the most important piece of the equation, and "me" continues to be the common denominator. Even when you are deflated, you are paying attention to you!

Brene Brown is a shame expert. She is the first researcher to have a filmed talk on Netflix. Her Ted Talk has been viewed over 35 million times. She speaks to those who see themselves as leaders about needing courage and creativity to change the world for good. Specifically, she encourages her audience to put themselves in a vulnerable spot. According to Brown,

> When you walk into that arena and you think, "I am going to try this," shame is the gremlin who says, "Uh, uh, you're not good enough. You never finished your MBA. Your wife left you. I know your dad really wasn't in Luxembourg, he was in Sing Sing. I know those things that happened to you growing up. I know you don't

think you're pretty, smart, talented, or powerful enough. I know your dad never paid attention, even when you made CFO." Shame is that thing.[27]

Brown states that shame says two things. First, it tells you that you're never good enough, and if you can talk it out of that one, it asks, "Who do you think you are?"[27] Those two phrases are representative of the two things we are getting at! We are either working to prove we are actually as good as we want others to see us, or we are failing to work in fear that, when we try, others will see all of our shortcomings. The questions above are offensive to us because we have settled on the fact we are at the center of our universe. There is a confrontation which has to occur, and we have to see it. We primarily work to take care of our fragile selves. That is why I had to be confronted where my pride lay, that gremlin saying, "You will never live up."

There are hundreds of books that tell you how to fight those gremlins. Not this one. There are hundreds of coaches and self-help experts who will teach you how to tell yourself you really are good enough. Not this one. I am offering a new direction, and I believe a more sustainable direction. What if we just agreed with the gremlin? What if we agree because we have accepted the confrontation that we can never be good enough?

I told you from the onset, I want to change the questions we are asking that define our success. If we can see the assumptions that hold up the questions the gremlins of shame are asking, we may not even see the need to refute them. We may stop having to say, "Yes I am good enough" or "I am somebody."

Before I show you how that could happen, let's acknowledge that we already know how powerful underlying assumptions are when asking questions or making statements. In sales, you learn you never ask, "Would you like to buy?", but rather, you ask, "Which product would you prefer, A or B?" The assumption is that you are going to buy something, the salesman just needs to know which one.

We had a massive storm in our area, and I was telling my friend how angry people were when we could not get an adjuster to their home the next day. He laughed and said, "You should explain the adjusters are helping other clients with more damage." The assumption was if people knew why there was no adjuster, they would not be as angry. That assumption was wrong, by the way.

This is why when someone asks me why the adjuster has not called, or why their rate goes up, or why we did anything they do not approve of, I always ask the same question. Do you really want to know why, or are you just mad at me? I have learned to ask that because sometimes going at the question is more powerful in getting at truth than trying to answer the question as it stands.

What if, at work, we just said ok to the gremlins of shame? What if we just go ahead and admit we are not as good as we once thought? What if we go ahead and admit we are not as different or innovative as we once thought? What if we threw out the worst to first way of thinking altogether? I know if we did not replace that mindset with a better one, we would be paralyzed. If we decided that we were no longer going to work to gain significance or money or make a name for ourselves primarily, we would need a new model to work from. It's time to make the decision to go *Last to Least*. It's costly, but it's worth it!

The confrontation obviously does not say you are just fine the way you are, and I am just fine the way I am, so let's just let each other live our own lives. It's not opposite either, that I am not ok, so I want to be like you, or, you are not ok, so you should be like me. The confrontation says none of us are fine ON OUR OWN. That is the point!

If we want a full and beautiful life, there are others we have to lean on. We cannot accomplish everything we want without the work of all community members, even those who perform jobs we think of as menial tasks. In fact, we probably need them the most! Worst to first means you have to work in a way that moves you ahead of others in the rankings, and we see the harm to the marketplace this thought process causes. When I step from worst to first, I automatically have to knock someone else down from number one. I am all for upward mobility of the entire group, but logically going worst to first must decrease someone else's ranking in the system.

Remember, this is SELF-management. I can imagine a reader thinking this sounds like a wimpy way to eliminate competition. It is not. *Last to Least* could never be demanded from someone else, because it is a system of self-management. Nobody really knows how you manage yourself, and nobody gets to determine that but you. To leave this old worst to first way of thinking behind demands free choice.

Think about stripping the gremlin of shame of his power when he says, "You are not good enough." Your response could be, "I know, so what?" Or when he asks, "Who do you think you are?" and you are able to respond, "It's not about me, so I don't think I am anybody." Some of us cannot imagine setting out to work hard and take on the challenges of the marketplace with those weak answers. We often realize that these answers are true, but we are worried that we will miss out on our best lives if we acknowledge those truths. Many have had the courage, or at least curiosity, to try out this upside-down view.

It's not a new concept! As diverse a crowd as Jesus and even rapper Eminem have taught this wisdom. Jesus called his followers to die to themselves. There is not a much more vivid picture of a confrontation where your own self-interests are put aside for some greater reason! Roger Ebert describes Eminem's character, "Rabbit" in the movie *8 Mile* saying, "The genius of Rabbit is to admit his own weaknesses!"

Have you seen *8 Mile*?[28] The storyline twists around rap battles between inner city young men. The purpose of a rap battle, if you are unfamiliar, is to shame the other person you are battling with an onslaught of rhyming words. In the final rap battle of the movie, Rabbit squares off with the best rapper in town, with whom who he has been in constant conflict throughout the movie. Warning: It is pretty graphic. I have typed 10 sentences to explain the storyline, but I deleted each one. Every sentence I deleted sounds either too graphic, or like I am not getting at the heart of the movie. I think that helps you see what kinds of conflict I am talking about.

In that final battle Rabbit goes first. The genius that Roger Ebert is talking about is that Rabbit goes ahead and says everything about himself he knows his opponent will use against him. What do you say to a man who has just committed rap-battle suicide? You cannot say anything, he is dead! And that is exactly what happened. The music started and the best rapper in town froze up, the worst possible embarrassment in this fictitious shame and honor rap-battle world.

Can you see the wisdom in dying to yourself? There is wisdom in saying to the gremlins, "You are correct, I am not good enough." There is freedom in admitting, "I am not the smartest." We can be led to realize, "I am not the center, but there is a beautiful place for even me." We do not have to convince the gremlins, or anyone else, that we are someone special if we just agree that we are not.

Think about how amazing it could be to work if I didn't have to constantly prove to the gremlins, my coworkers, or my family that I am indeed valuable. Think about the attention to productivity and lack of distraction if I am working like someone who has died when it comes to recognition or approval?

I got there. I am not trying to be melodramatic, but I got to the point where I lay in my bed night after night thinking about the real meaning of life. I realized my work could NOT be about making a name for myself, or making more money, or even the "Christian" version, "I JUST wanted to provide for my family." I say "Christian" because this is not the version of work Jesus prescribed. However, I have heard people say they just need to provide for their family as a reason to work. If my families' provision is the only reason or even the main reason I work, I am overemphasizing some things Christianity teaches and underemphasizing others. Simply providing for my family is not the guiding principle of work for Paul the apostle. I knew I couldn't work that way. I lay in my bed and thought, "Let's get it over with. Let's see behind the curtain and see if there is really a life after death or not. If there is nothing more to live for, then let's just get it over with!" I am glad to say I found a better way. Work is not simply about dying to some things, it is about working FOR other things.

That is why you need to replace the worst to first mindset rather than just eliminate it. If you just eliminate your purpose for working, you will be left feeling empty and directionless. It starts with the confrontation to admit our weaknesses and our true purpose for work. Yes, you want to provide, yes, you want a fulfilling job that allows you to pursue your passions, but there is MORE—a bigger bottom line than profit! The shift comes when you stop working for your own interests and begin working for the interests of others.

I have heard the naysayers before. Chip heard me, but there were others who said, "I thought you would have more than that?" and "I thought you had a magic bullet!" This simple concept will change your work in a massive way, but it is costly. You do have to have the courage of Jesus. You have to die to worst to first!

You may not be fully convinced of going *Last to Least*, but I think you have to admit going back to worst to first is out of the question. It is an endless spiral into selfishness that will ultimately leave you feeling empty. We need something stronger than our individual efforts to hold us all up! We need a community!

We need to all choose to go *Last to Least*!

PART 5

WHAT IS *LAST TO LEAST?*

There is a social scientist who is Professor Emeritus from Princeton University named Sam Glucksberg. I heard about his research with about 14 million others in a TED talk by Dan Pink. Dan Pink was speaking about motivation and Glucksberg's research helped him make a great point. Glucksberg had researched motivation in doing two types of tasks.[29] In an interview, Glucksberg explains the research and outlines the task types. One, a task that is straightforward and the solution is obvious and two, a task where the solution is not what you think at first. He used the famous candle problem to study people's responses. Participants are given a candle and a box of tacks. They are asked to fix the candle to the wall in such a way that, when lit, the wax from the candle will not get on the table. In the easier version, the tacks are on the table and the box is empty. In the more difficult version, the tacks are in the box. Seeing the tacks in the box makes it difficult because participants see the box as only a tack holder, not part of the solution.

The solution is to tack the box to the wall and then put the candle in the box.

Predictably, he found that incentive caused people to finish the problem with the obvious solution much faster. Surprisingly, though, he found that the incentive decreased effectiveness when the problem called for a more creative solution! Glucksberg's research disproved the conventional wisdom regarding incentives. Self-centered incentives are not only ineffective, they are actually counterproductive to solving the most difficult problems. Isn't that true in so many facets of life that the best way is not obvious? Don't so many of the wisest solutions turn out to be counterintuitive? So it is with *Last to Least*! We instinctively think that if we want to be happy and fulfilled, we have to go worst to first. We intuitively believe that we need to focus on, "What is in it for me?" to make us most productive. This is why we tether ourselves to these purposes. We are tied to MY money, MY approval, MY comfort. Glucksberg is showing us that we work best when we focus on the work itself and not simply what benefits the work brings to me!

Glucksberg's research is proof that working with my benefits as the guide to managing myself is counterproductive. Remember, though, we cannot simply remove worst to first working, we have to replace it.

Dan Pink not only has a popular Ted Talk on motivation, he also wrote one of the most helpful sales books I have ever read. *To Sell is Human* argues that almost every job in today's economy is selling.[30] He shows how those in medicine and education are selling ideas. He shows us how all small businesses begin with the owners having to sell. Census data shows that one in nine people are in a sales job, but he argues that today, so are the other eight.

We are all in sales and we have all adopted the idea that "more incentive equals more production." Except, it does not. We are all in sales and we are shouting at ourselves like a used car manager "get out there and the money will flow in." We are all in sales, and we are like an insurance sales manager prodding ourselves to work harder for a bonus that is just in our reach. Glucksberg is showing us that we do not actually achieve better results steering ourselves this way.

Those in sales have accepted that incentive equals production, and we are our own managers. This is the more and more era that Peter Drucker spoke of in the late 90's when he said, "more and more knowledge workers must learn to manage themselves."[31] We are managing ourselves to sell our ideas, products, services, but we must change the guiding principle or we will actually be less likely to sell AND less likely to get the incentive we desire.

David Foster Wallace reminded us we do not get to choose IF we worship, only WHO or WHAT we worship. Let me be clear. I am NOT saying that meeting needs with our work is what we should worship. If we choose work as the guiding principle of our entire life, we will be as disappointed as some of those who choose power or beauty. Work is not a good center for life. The connection to Wallace's quote is that just as we must choose a center for life, we must choose a center for work. In life, we will choose a guide to follow at every turn. At work, we will choose a guide for every turn. I am not suggesting a guide for all of life. There are sometimes when my family comes before my work. There are times when I could be more productive but choose to rest. David Foster Wallace actually says that the reason people choose a higher power to worship is because everything else will eat you alive. If you worship work, it will eat you alive.

Glucksberg helps us see what is unproductive: my needs guiding my work. That does not tell us how to steer ourselves, it only confirms that self-self-centered work is less productive. What should we allow to guide us then?

Let's look at the counterintuitive way we were meant to work. We will enjoy the beauty of *Last to Least* from all sides, so I will try to say what it is a few different ways, but each will need some clarification because of the way our brains have been trained to hear these phrases.

THE THREE QUESTIONS

When nobody else is watching, and nobody else will even know what I am thinking, I must be able to manage myself. If I can learn to answer three questions, I can become an excellent self manager.

1. What is the guiding purpose of my work?

2. Who achieves this purpose?

3. How do I do it?

The order matters as much as the questions, and I will show you why in the next section. These three simple questions serve as a framework to manage yourself when you are asked to be creative and do things that nobody has done before. They will guide you when you need to remain focused on a task you have done thousands of times, but know it must be done. These questions can provide you with a steady hand and a passionate heart to do both the most daring or what seems like the most boring assignments. They focus our attention, they clarify our purpose, and inspire our creativity.

QUESTION #1:
WHAT IS THE GUIDING PURPOSE OF WORK.

Until now, we have talked about what the purpose *is not*. The guiding purpose of work in the *Last to Least* system is meeting needs. Meeting needs necessarily precedes any benefit from work that comes back to me. There are no profits generated until a need is met. I cannot be paid without meeting a need. I cannot be recognized for my work until a need is met. I will not be approved by others until a need is met. It is terribly obvious. Yet, I ask groups everywhere I travel, "Why do you work so hard?" and I almost never hear, "To meet a need." I was giving a talk to a college basketball team recently. I asked them, "Why do you work so hard?" They gave the common answers: money, sense of accomplishment, etc.

I asked one of the players to imagine I was selling him a product. What if I said, "You should buy this product because I will make money. Would you like to buy it?" Of course, he said no. "Oh, but it will also give me a sense of accomplishment to sell it to you. Are you ready now?"

This may sound silly to you, but why do we lead ourselves through work as if people are there to give us what we need and want? Could this be the reason we are so unproductive and disengaged? We are thinking about the purpose of our work incorrectly and wrong thoughts lead to wrong actions. We have to align our thoughts with what is true about work and then we can lead ourselves through the weeds productively. That's why *Last to Least* is a neighbors-guided system of self management.

WHAT DOES NEIGHBORS-GUIDED MEAN?

Our neighbors are no longer the people who sleep close to us. Now that traveling hundreds of miles has become simple, our neighbor can be across the planet. Neighbor has always been a term that describes "someone living near us." The definition is the same here, but where we "live" has changed. So much "living" is done away from where we sleep now. We may work miles away or at least do business with those far from our homes. Our work is serving people across the earth, so "someone living near us" could be someone "living" in the same online community as us! Neighbors-guided work keeps us from moving toward money or possessions or comfort to the detriment of the people the work is designed to serve.

Even if we have been guided by money, possessions, or approval, there is still a neighbor at the end of the line who makes that possible! You have to make a trade with your "neighbor" before your work can make you the money, get you the approval, earn the comfort. It is not money that simply appears in your check. The money is PAID BY someone. The person paying is a client, customer; I am calling them a "neighbor." No money is paid until a need is met somewhere down the line.

Last to Least is simply making "ME" the least important and my neighbor the most important. *Last to Least* is tethering to the needs of my neighbor and allowing that relationship to keep me from moving too far in my quest for the other purposes of work. For some who have worked for another purpose for so long, it is shocking to even realize your neighbor is still in the picture! A teacher doing money-guided work can forget he is only paid because a student needs to learn. A salesman working to make a name for himself is only acclaimed if some neighbor writes a check for the product being sold. A hospital executive whose every move is made to make sure he is recognized as a leader in the industry is still dependent on patients paying bills. If they do not pay for your work, you will not be paid, recognized, or approved.

I have a friend who was educated in the Milton Friedman era of "The Only Social Responsibility of Money is Shareholder Profit." When I tried to explain the concept of a neighbors-guided approach to work, he scoffed at the idea. He brought me back to the simple exchanges that I illustrated about trading work. "If my family is going to starve," he said, "I do not care about my neighbor. I just want him to give me some corn, so I give him a lamb." I understand his point completely, but it was as if he had NEVER considered that the neighbor to whom he was selling the lamb had a choice. That neighbor could choose to buy the lamb from someone else. If I am solving a problem for him by providing the lamb in a way that addressed his needs, he might choose me over another supplier or even give me a little more corn. Either way, unless I give him something he wants, I can never get my returns. Even if I keep money at the center, my neighbor is still in the picture. I may not care one bit about his needs, but I still have to get the corn from the farmer or the money from a customer today before "working for money" makes any sense at all.

Even if we cannot see that managing ourselves with money at the center is not the best way to work, surely we see that our neighbors needs are in the formula. *Last to Least* is not forgetting money any more than someone working for money can forget their neighbor. It is finding a new center by which to manage ourselves and our decisions. *Last to Least* is turning from worrying about being in first or last place and focusing instead on becoming the least important, while making my neighbors' needs most important. Neighbors-guided work is the aim.

"Neighbors-guided" is my term. I do think you will agree the term "neighbors-guided" gets to the heart of *Last to Least* more than client, or customer, or even patient-centered in the medical world. The other words allow the person my work serves the distinct disservice of putting themselves at the center as well. It does not allow them to appreciate the community they enjoy as a variable in the work I am providing.

Don't you want to do business with someone who places the needs of you and your community at the center of what they do? Wouldn't you like to see a *Last to Least* certification seal on the door of your doctor's office, or dentist, or insurance agent? Wouldn't that make you feel confident that they cared enough to train their team to work with you and your neighbors in mind?

MANAGING YOURSELF

Peter Drucker coined the term, "knowledge worker" in 1999. He used the word to refer to people who work with their minds more than their backs. He said, "more and more knowledge workers must learn to manage themselves."[31] In 2008 Harvard Business review reprinted a chapter from his book on management principles and called it "Managing Oneself."[32] *Last to Least* can be best understood as a system of self-management. With so many leadership books agreeing that self-management is a prerequisite to leadership, I was shocked at how few attempts there are to actually give us guidance on the matter.

"Just get out there and do it," is not enough. "Work hard" is too vague. "Figure it out" is not actually helping someone develop the important skill of self-management that is required before one is capable of leading others. I hope it is now clear that we are either managing ourselves by choosing a central, guiding purpose or we are being managed unwittingly. When we are able to tie every action, every plan, and every vision back to the neighbors that our work is made to serve, we are able to make wise, honest, and informed decisions. In a complex and creative work environment, it is the needs of the neighbors we serve and the neighbors our work affects that keep our minds sharply focused. Neighbors-guided work keeps us from making decisions that are short-sighted and narrowly focused and keeps us thinking about what can be sustained and is mutually beneficial to all parties.

"Why not help neighbors *and* help myself?" That is a common question and a good one. And I say yes, do both always. I just know that there will be times when there will be a conflict of interest. Just consider the new and creative ways to make money and be recognized that would emerge if we centered our work around our neighbors. I wonder how many amazing ideas we have missed out on because our best and brightest minds took the route to money at the expense of their neighbors' needs when they could have kept brainstorming and created an idea that would do both! If I commit to managing myself with neighbors as the most important variable, it may be more difficult and may challenge me more, but why settle for less?

Neighbors-guided self-management literally changes everything. It gives me clarity of purpose that I can easily communicate to inspire cooperation and a sense of purpose and drive even when the tasks seem mundane. Every great accomplishment comes with some tasks that are not glamorous. A neighbors-guided approach gives me poise under pressure because I have forgotten myself and am not plagued with my own fears and anxieties. The gremlins we learned about from Brene Brown are silenced. It keeps me safe from ethical violations that could waste resources or result in termination or worse. It keeps me from having to cover up decisions that cost me valuable time today and later. It gives me the freedom to admit where I am powerless, so I can focus on what I can actually influence. *Last to Least* gives me everything I need to manage myself when there are so many other opinions fighting for my allegiance. The more the market demands creativity, the more self-management will separate the successful from the failures.

IDENTIFYING THE TRUE MEANS AND ENDS

I enjoy reading philosophy because, like most of us, I grew up in a community where ideas were guarded. That is not intended to be a negative or positive statement, but most of us see "our way" as "the way" and protect those we love from outside ideas. If we are not careful, questions about our deeply-held beliefs are seen as obnoxious and defiant. "If it was good enough for grandpa, it's good enough for me," was not a punchline in my community, it was a line of logic that was accepted as a bedrock. Although I enjoy learning different ideas, those ideas have their own blind spots. What I have learned is philosophy is in a tough spot right now. I learned a lot from reading *A Brief History of Thought* by Luc Ferry. He breaks philosophy down broadly by saying it is concerned with three elements:[33]

1. Theory about origins and purpose of life

2. Ethics about how to treat others

3. Wisdom or salvation about what gives us contentment and freedom from fear.

Ferry then takes the major turns in recorded history and shows the way the philosophical "eras" addressed these elements. Ferry begins with ancient thought and Greek Stoicism, then turns to Christian thought, then modern thought brought about by the Enlightenment, then Postmodern thought lead by Nietzsche, Freud, and Marx, then on to contemporary philosophy. He showed how each era addressed the elements of theory, ethics, and salvation differently. He evoked the thoughts of Heidegger to explain our current state.

I am not qualified to break down Luc Ferry's assessment of Heidegger, but I will try to explain because it will help us understand means and ends clearly. For all of time there have been ends and means. In the past I explained that I worked hard SO I could get a vacation. The thing you are doing is obviously the "means" and the result you hope for is the "ends."

Heidegger, according to Luc Ferry, rationalized that humanity had embraced the means by which we formerly achieved an end as ends themselves. They use the examples of technology. There is no reason we try to buy the latest Apple product other than because it is the latest model. He brings to light that formerly we wanted the newest gadget or wanted to progress BECAUSE it made us happier or BECAUSE it helped us live longer. The reason now is simply BECAUSE you will have the latest gadget. Progress in technology was a means to an end, but now is simply an end in itself. Heidegger is considered one of the most intelligent contemporary philosophers and the most important according to Luc Ferry, even though

Heidegger was a supporter of Nazism. To be fair, I think Ferry was praising Heidegger for his diagnosis, not his prescription.

The ends and means have not simply been confused, but the lines between them have been blurred. The reason for this blurring of the lines is deconstruction. Deconstruction tries to strip meaning from ideas and words. If you say, "you should work hard," a good deconstructionist would respond, "You sound confident, what makes you so sure of that?" Each response you give would be met with the same question. The deconstructionist is trying to show you that your ideas is ultimately based on something you cannot "know." Without going into much more philosophy, deconstructionists believe that our origins cannot be known. We saw from Plantigna's work that without being confident of origin, we cannot be confident about purpose. See? These ideas are formulated in universities, but they make it to the streets. When they make it to the streets, they are often disconnected from their origin. That is part of a deconstructionists theory and also paramount to understanding them.

I was reading *A Brief History of Thought* while at the beach with my three brothers, their wives, our children, and my parents. We were all out on the beach in Hilton Head in the afternoon. I know it was the afternoon because I was reading. In the morning all the kids are out, so there is not time for reading, but my dad hates the beach so in the afternoons he stays back while some of the kids nap, and we have a little adult time. I think all the wives were reading about Chip and Jojo from HGTV's *Fixer Upper*, and two of the three brothers were asleep. I'm sure my mom was tanning and reading Sandra Brown. There was little interest in my reading choice, and I was well aware— because I had tried to start a few philosophical conversations with the group with very little success. Then I read this part and got their attention. "This stuff makes it to Gillsville!" I shouted as I sprang from my chair. Gillsville is the northeast Georgia town where we grew up, and not exactly a hotbed of philosophical thought. Most people I know could care less about Heidegger, Ferry, or Plantigna. These philosophical tools are seen as common sense, though, even in Gillsville. Even in your community, even in your own mind, even if you never acknowledge it. That is why thinking about these things can be so powerful. We need to determine our current operating system if we ever intend to change or improve.

My family group is acclimated to my "discoveries," so I hardly woke up one brother and was no match for the Magnolia story! But, it's true, Nietzsche had made it to Gillsville.

I did not realize the depth to which deconstruction had moved into the assumptions of my generation. We think skepticism is a virtue! "Who says?" is a way to define intelligence. I will never forget my "gifted" teacher announcing to our class that "the smart students answer the questions, but the gifted students question the answers." We took that line all the way. We question everything!

And if we are good deconstructionists, then we are dangerously close to forgetting the difference between the means and the ends to these means. I am trying to acknowledge where these issues come from as a way to provide us a better direction forward. I want you to rethink some of the "common sense" you may have accepted.

Going *Last to Least* is a model of working for the good of neighbors as an end and positioning all the tactics and strategies we learn as means for their good. To make the philosophical practical, if neighbors are ends, not means, then a doctor practices because her neighbor has cancer, not only because the fees pay her mortgage. A teacher educates because his students need to become familiar with

the scientific process, not because he needs a secure job while trying
to be published. A start-up begins, not as a way to gain followers, but
as a way to meet needs.

SACRIFICING THE SELF

Luc Ferry, Deepak Chopra, Oprah, Brene Brown and even Chip
and Jojo are all people who modern people turn to help define the
meaning of life. And all of these people have one thing in common.
They believe love is the way to get where we want to go. Deepak
Chopra says,

> We need to restore love as the key to happiness—a
> difficult task...We see all around us people who madly
> pursue pleasure, or money, or status because they don't
> trust in love. Without such trust that love can make a
> difference, of course you will pursue surrogates. Pleasure,
> money, and status are compensations when love is absent
> or too weak to transform your life. [34]

We were asked to define love at a gathering I was attending a few
years ago. I think this definition gets to the heart of *Last to Least*.
Love is self-sacrifice for another whose good brings you more joy
than what you gave up. *Last to Least* is embracing true humility in
my work. Rick Warren, author of world famous *The Purpose Driven
Life*, said humility was not thinking less of ourselves, but thinking
of ourselves less.[35] This sentence has changed my work, and it could
change yours as well. It changed Chip, the agent at my first office, and
others who have embraced it. When I take myself out of the center

of the equation in my work, I can focus the attention where it should be—the person, client, customer, the NEIGHBORS that my work was created to serve. Chopra points out that I will not need the other self-pleasing motivations for work when I can embrace loving my neighbor. Obviously, this is not romantic love. This is genuine care and service for those who our work was created to serve.

I believe neighbors-guided work is the calling of the progressive. Self-centered work has caused enough problems because we have an injured identity. Think about it. We are rarely aware of our big toe, but it is just there, doing its job. But, our egos, ourselves, we are constantly aware of. If our identities were not injured, we would have a personal experience more like a big toe. We would exist and do our part, but not be so aware of our wounds. Our egos are more like a stubbed toe than a normal well-functioning one. I want to work like a proper big toe, staying out of my own way. I want to work for the good of someone else and not worry about myself so much. I want to consider the interests of others and not just my own. Let's go from focusing on LAST place or worst to considering ourselves LEAST important. I want to go from *Last to Least*. So, to reconsider the sentence I proposed as a definition of love, let's take a look.

Last to Least is self-sacrifice. All work really is costly to the worker. The mental or physical energy involved in work costs us. The time you spend working could obviously be spent on other things. When you leverage resources in finance to invest in an idea or business, there is a cost. When you invest that money, it could have been used for more toys or immediate returns. The teacher gives himself emotionally to his students and that same energy could have been used elsewhere. The dental lab owner sacrifices a day away camping because two dentists call with an order hours before he planned to leave.

This means there is truly a cost to *Last to Least*. Honestly, if you skip a rock across the material out there about self-sacrifice, the authors are warning us not to sacrifice too much. They are saying be careful how much you sacrifice yourself because you will burn out! In a presentation overseas one of the first questions I was asked by a master's level counselor working on his Ph.D was, "What about self-care?" He gave me the example of another counselor he knew who burned out quickly after giving too much without taking time for himself. His point was that self-care would have kept his friend from burning out. I wanted to ask what specifically caused the burnout. Was it really from trying too hard to meet the needs of others, or was there something else at the center? Were you really trying to make your clients a means to your end? Was it their needs, or you being their savior that was at the center?

I am not saying we should allow people to use and abuse us. Big toes do not let the rest of the body take advantage of them. Allowing others to take advantage of us is not managing ourselves. In fact, it shows a lack of self-management because we allow ourselves to be taken hostage by feelings of guilt, then resentment. Those feelings quickly lead right back to placing ourselves in the center once again. When we are unwilling to confront someone who we feel may be taking advantage, we are often not looking out for their best interests, but our own unwillingness to have healthy conflict.

Is it truly neighbors-guided to allow someone to take advantage of us time and time again? Is it really good for a client to be allowed to be overwhelmingly self-centered? Will this not lead to the shrinking of their own desire to work for others? At the very least, it will be detrimental to the other neighbors we serve. In a specialized economy, the way I can be a service to the community is to be able to serve multiple members of the community in a specialized area. If I allow one community member to monopolize my time, is that neighbors-guided? Definitely not. Giving one person all your energy or more energy than you can sustain will lead to a cycle of crippling negative emotions, ultimately benefitting no one. Proper self-management requires the humility to admit we are not powerful enough to meet every need. At the same time, if we cry "self-care" every time we are uncomfortable, we are probably either lazy or self-centered and want to place ourselves back in the center with our martyrdom.

Last to Least is not boosting your own pride with feelings of martyrdom. Rather, it is self-sacrifice for the good of another! The sacrifice was never the main point. If the sacrifice becomes the main point, then we are missing *Last to Least*. The good of another is the main goal of *Last to Least*. I would like for you to pause and think of some ways your work is for the good of another. This takes some tough work. As an example, I will use my own profession. I hope it will help you get to the bottom of the way you can help others.

You may think you are not a salesman, but according to Dan Pink we are all selling. He says, "Yes, one in nine Americans works in sales. *But so do the other eight.* Whether we're employees pitching colleagues on a new idea, entrepreneurs enticing funders to invest, or parents and teachers cajoling children to study, we spend our days trying to move others. Like it or not, we're all in sales now.[30]

We can apply these same principles to those we are trying to "move". If we are doing a great job of serving people, we are often trying to influence them, so these sales examples should translate into trying to move students to perform on tests, move patients to progress in their health, or move peoples to spend resources on our products instead of whatever they were going to spend it on.

How do you sell insurance for the good of others? If I ask that question to your agent, he would probably say he should not lie and that would be the extent. When work is about getting money, the only other factor is, "Is it legal?" Of course, we should obey the law, but how can we truly do good for people?

Selling can be a service. A follow-up to *Last to Least* could be "Serve by Selling." There is a great opportunity to take advantage or to serve, especially with a product people do not know much about. I sell life insurance to many clients who have little knowledge about the product. I answered the phone one day and a client who had business with me (whom I barely knew) asked for some quotes on life insurance. She said she wanted to compare what she had through work, and I asked if we could meet to discuss it. Selling is transferring what I believe to you. When you believe what I believe, the next step of purchasing my product is obvious, It is difficult to transfer belief over the phone, so I like face-to-face meetings.

Again, if I truly believe she needs to better understand her choices, my request for a face-to-face interview is not just a better way to sell, but a better way to serve her. She agreed to the interview and when she arrived, I was ready to work with some questions to put her interests above my own. When we were finished, she looked at me fiercely, piercing me with her gaze.

"Thank you!" she said with emotion. "I have never understood what life insurance is all about, and you have made it perfectly clear!"

This client had likely never experienced an agent who worked to help her understand her options rather than just to make a sale. Work should be about love, not selfishness or money. All of these beautiful ideas are usually met with skepticism and cross looks more than anything else. I am an idealist, but even I was shocked to end a sales presentation with such a heartfelt thanks. I actually got a little uncomfortable, and I pride myself on being comfortable in uncomfortable situations.

I was giving myself and my education to this lady with her benefit in mind. I admit, it is easy to sacrifice yourself when it turns out you made the sale or landed the client, but what about if you do not? There are many times when the *Last to Least* approach is recognized and appreciated, but there are other times there is no external reward. In those cases, when you are guided only by serving the needs of others, you will still have achieved your purpose.

I have another example of an incident that did not work out as well. This is where you find out if you are committed to *Last to Least*, or if you are just using it as a means to really go worst to first. Every sales company has hurdles to jump and goals to meet, and my business is no different. Sometimes meeting a certain sales target can be very beneficial to me and my family. This time the benefit was high, and I was one application away from hitting the mark. To complicate matters, when I say high benefit, I am talking significant here. All my other requirements were met, but I needed one application. I sold the one application to a client who already had a policy with us. It was in her best interest to change to different type coverage, and she was going to be in a better position. I left on the last day of the year feeling great about helping my client and reaping the rewards that come from passing the hurdle.

Later at home I received a call. It was from my home office. They called to say if they waited to process the application until January 2nd, the client would receive a dividend payment on the old policy and still benefit from the new. If I had known even hours earlier, I could have contacted the client or even tried to find another application, but because it was 20 minutes before closing, I was out of time. I had to either allow the client to receive the small dividend and lose out on a large compensation bonus or go ahead without the client ever knowing and reap my rewards. The client would have never known the difference. She had already agreed to the terms without knowing about the dividend.

I was doing work with a college team recently and told this story. When I got to this part I paused dramatically. "What do you think I did?" I asked. They were hanging on the edge of their seats.

I said, "I told them to put that through because I gotta get that money".

One guy in the back pumped his fist. He was so happy I had been talking about taking care of others, but that I had taken care of myself this time. Almost as if he was like, "Yes, I knew he didn't mean he does this all the time." And that is true, I did tell them to put it through without telling the client.

But, I hung up the phone and I immediately felt sick. At this time, I had not thought of the phrase *Last to Least*, but I was already trying to practice the concept and even had started to share it as my way to success. When I hung up the phone, I remembered Philippians 2: "Look not only to your own interests, but also look to the interests of others."

I picked up the phone and called the home office and stopped them from putting my interests above the clients. We were on the way to a New Year's Eve party a few minutes later, and I could have cried. The thought of losing the bonus and the admiration of my wife and colleagues that came along with it was a heavy burden.

When the stakes are high, the self-sacrifice is not just chatter. There is some real pain. I was telling my wife about the sadness and disappointment, and I was really hoping she was not disappointed in me. The sacrifice cost her as well!

She said, "You would have been miserable if you had done that." She knew that the neighbors-guided approach would keep me from guilt and regret, and I could truly enjoy the successes when they came. The neighbors-guided approach provided a true north when the directions of my moral compass were out of alignment. Imagine if I had been tethered to money or comfort, what a difference it would have made.

I cannot make you understand the look on Chip's face when I told him what I had done. I had only been in that new office, for 2 months when this occurred. I am convinced that this jewel of a moment gave me the opportunity to show him that I was serious about meeting needs over profits. It provided him a perfect illustration and I know if he would have made his massive turnaround without it.

Here is another illustration from the insurance business to help you see. There are many times I have explained what insurance really is when I am questioned about rate increases. I am careful to explain the only way we are able to pay claims is with the premiums we collect from your neighbor. Insurance companies gain from investment income, but there is nothing to invest without premium dollars from the members. Early on I would say what I was taught, "When claims go up, premiums have to go up." Now that I have learned to explain that thoroughly, there are many fewer outbursts, but about once a week, the same eruption occurs that I was used to every time before. "I haven't had a claim! Why do I have to pay for them?" The answer to that question is actually extremely simple. "That is the only way insurance is possible."

Really smart people ask me that question all the time. I am

convinced it is not a reflection of their aptitude, but a subtle look into the "client-focused" definitions of work we have internalized. If I focus on the perceived needs of my current client with no regard to other clients, I cannot answer "What is my contribution?" to the fullest. My contribution is not relegated to the person in front of me, but also the community in which we find ourselves. This overemphasis causes my clients to be upset when their neighbors effect their own premiums. I can only imagine how this works in education. If there were other students in the classroom who needed a slower pace than your child, do you expect the teacher to move ahead for your own child or take the time others need? Teachers must take the classroom into consideration, not just the student. Real estate investors must take the community into consideration, not simply their own developments, at least if everyone is going to thrive.

There is a major difference between client-centered and neighbors-guided. Client-centered means the needs of the individual client come first, whereas neighbors-guided takes the individual into account, but also factors in the needs of the community as a whole. The hyper focus of a client-centered approach has already had detrimental effects in the medical world. My first rotation as a newly educated PA student was where I learned what we "really do." The practitioner I worked with told me he was prescribing a Z-pac (an antibiotic) for a client we just saw with a runny nose. I had not learned my lessons in respecting authority, so I bluntly challenged him. "That is probably a virus and a Z-pac will not do anything for a virus. Won't that lead to mutation and resistance in the community?" As tactless as I was, I was actually touting correct information, and he agreed. "They think it works," he said, "So if I don't give it to them, they will just get it from somewhere else." This is a client-centered approach.

I would like to see communities flourishing with workers taking a neighbors-guided approach. When we are steered by meeting needs, we even confront someone when they are wrong instead of giving in. We help them to understand how to meet their true needs, even when those needs are different than what the person thought they were like the example above. *Last to Least* is self-sacrifice for the good of others, not just the client you are presently serving, but the neighbors you both live with.

Last to Least is self-sacrifice for the good of another whose benefit brings you more pleasure than what you gave up! The self-sacrifice was tough for sure, but it would have hurt even more if I had put my own interests first. My wife was right. My neighbor's benefit gave me more pleasure than the bonus would have given me at her expense. I heard John Piper speaking about love in this way once.[36] Piper has written 50 books and sold millions of copies. Many of these books are about finding true joy in true love. He asked a question. "What if I brought my wife home flowers and she lavished me with thanks and praise and gratitude? What if my response to her exuberance was, 'Well I had to do it because it was your birthday!' Would she experience my love, or would the weight of my duty crush her spirit?" Then he answered, "She would rather know that it was my pleasure to sacrifice my money for her benefit!"

I am sure that when you work for the good of others, there is not always a shower of thanks coming your way. Just imagine a community filled with people who have a neighbors-guided mindset. You would not have to be selfish because as you worked for the good of others they would be simultaneously looking out for your interests. Someone has to start it—could it be you?

Last to Least is not only a way to look to the interests of other individuals, but it is also a way to look to the needs of a community. As I have repeatedly said, I am an insurance man. One of the most difficult tasks I have is explaining rate increases. We think very individualistically, so when we are charged as a group, we have a hard time understanding. The way I explain it is that if four people started "*Last to Least* Insurance Group" they would all put their money into a common pool.

For example, let's say they each built a barn and wanted to insure it for $4,000. They would each put $1,000 into the pool and if one of their barns burned down, they would all agree the unfortunate person would get the $4,000 to rebuild. The pool would be replenished by everyone paying $1000, and the process starts over. However, if there was a year where two barns burned, they would have to each put $2,000 into the pool the next year!

So, when we have excessive claims, we have to increase rates, I explain. Still, they say, "Well, I didn't have a claim, so why am I getting charged?" If you think that is a valid question, I am not mad at you at all, because I have heard it a thousand times. I would ask you like I ask so many, "Do you really want to know why, or are you just mad at me?".

It is the same with risk selection. Do not let this bore you because this is not just about insurance. When we rate certain risks higher or lower, we have to do it on a population level, but it is applied to an individual. If you have a young driver in your household, you are not necessarily a higher risk as an individual family. However, 100 families with young drivers have a higher risk level than 100 families without young drivers. Because the overall population of families have a higher risk level, we have to charge the individual family more based on the population risk data.

We all have to go back and forth between thinking about how our work affects the individuals we interact with, but also the community in which we are a part. The way our work affects the community can be seen clearly with the housing bubble. Banks could look at an individual and say, "They may not be able to pay, but we can take a chance on them," but when they did that in massive numbers, the community suffered because of so many defaulted loans. They were not looking out for the best interests of the community, even if they had thoughts about getting the individual into a house.

I am sure there are some who think it is a dramatization to say their job is a service to anyone. I would encourage you to either connect those dots or try to find another vocation. While in college, I was a trash collector. I would ride on the back of a trash truck through the streets of the city of Lula, GA with Joel and Tony. Tony was a large man and had seniority, so he drove while Joel and I jumped on and off collecting garbage. Joel would scream, "Kick it Tony," every time we jumped back on and were safely holding the truck's handles. I thought I was just laughing at Joel and making enough to buy a little gas, but now that I have a home of my own, I realize how much of a service it is for my trash to be picked up. If we had to store our garbage on our property, our living conditions would be much worse. If I had to take my own garbage, I would miss out on valuable family time.

Do you make glasses? Do it so people can see, not so you can get paid. Do you fix cars? Do it so people can get where they need to be, not so you can be known as the best mechanic in town. Do you work an assembly line? Find out what your piece does to make the whole and who that whole serves in the end. When you wake up in the morning, think about the person being served by your diligence and work with that person in mind. When you are tired, think about the impact you are having on the community. Go *Last to Least*.

A NEW EQUATION FOR WINNING

I have seen more ads on social media promising to teach me to win (or as they put it, "10x") at life than pictures of cats. I do not care for either. Please do not hate me, cat lovers.

"10x=Win" is a popular equation for success. X equals my benefits. Someone living by this equation feels like they won whenever their benefits are multiplied by 10. Some people realize that there may be other considerations at play rather than just the self, so they may try living by a second equation: $10X + Y = Win$.

The X is still the most important variable, thus the multiplier of 10. But, they also see the need to be some benefit to others. Y equals the benefits of others. For people living by this equation to experience a win, they must 10X their own lives and be of some benefit to others.

Here is the new equation for winning when you are leading yourself according to *Last to Least*: $10Y + X = Win$. Do you see what happened? The benefits of others became the most valuable piece of the equation and my needs decreased in value. Someone living by this equation would feel like they only win if they maximize the benefits of others. The benefit to the self is secondary.

If this sounds insane to you, let me clarify: I do not think this new equation will decrease your results in our current economy. I am confident that those who truly learn to meet needs will benefit in the long run themselves. However, you cannot trick the process.

When leading myself, I cannot pretend I am meeting needs in order to win by the 10X. I am still living by the first equation. To live by the new equation, I have to seriously consider my needs as less valuable than the needs of my neighbors. This new equation has the potential to radically change communities and markets to operate with the efficacy of the systems of the human body. With each of us performing our unique role, the whole naturally enjoys maximum benefits.

A PREQUEL TO LEADERSHIP

The greatest prequel of all time is obviously *Batman Begins*.[37] My friend Kevin, who we call Turkey, was like kid on Christmas waiting for it to come out. He talked about it constantly and, though I was not a fan, his enthusiasm made me excited about its debut.

A prequel is so interesting because it tells the backstory to another story we have already found interesting and engaging. The prequel fills in the details about how characters developed and story lines developed, providing a new foundation from which to view all the stories we know so well.

Last to Least is a prequel to every leadership book...ever!

My first statement about the "greatest prequel of all time" was unsubstantiated. There is no source to quote for *Batman Begins* being the greatest prequel ever, only my opinion. However, open up your favorite leadership book and you will find the following in it. "Before you lead others, you must learn to lead yourself." There are a few ways the sentiment may be stated, but you will find it. Self-leadership or self-management is a well-acknowledged prerequisite to being an effective leader. *Last to Least* is the story before all the stories you read about leadership.

If the importance of self-management is so well acknowledged, why is there little material about the topic? I have a few good guesses, but instead of complaining about the lack of material, I decided to invoke my will to act. I wrote this book. That is what Ra's al Ghul told Master Bruce in *Batman Begins* as he was trying to teach him to cope with anger and guilt. "The will to act is everything!" Ghul admonishes. Here may be the key to why there is little self-leadership material. In the realm of self-leadership, the "will to act" is equivalent to limiting some of our freedoms. That scares us. We do not want less freedom.

If we decisively act, we are giving up the freedom to act differently. To say it another way. Assume X and Y are actions. If I cannot do X and Y simultaneously, I must choose one path and forsake another. It is a risk to choose a path. What if it's the wrong one? What scenery and experiences are we giving up by choosing one path over another? It's fear of missing out (or FOMO) at its finest.

I am not trying to be overly analytical, but I will be transparent to make this abundantly clear. I have been researching self–management for about five years now. I have spent hours codifying my system, writing it down, and revising it. I have spent money for people to do things that I have zero expertise in. They have designed the website, the cover, the internal pages. I have spent lots of time and money to act. I see a need and I am trying to meet that need in the market.

However, there is a chance that my action produces little fruit. I am not talking about ROI or book sales. I managed myself while writing *Last to Least* in the same way I encourage readers to manage themselves. I spent the hours reminding myself of the frustrated, disengaged manager who would read it and become energized and productive. I envisioned the small business owner disappointed that the growth had plateaued. I wrote the checks to those working with me, remembering that work brings up weeds and people need to hear these concepts.

However, there is a chance that none of these things happen. If there are no fruits (no one is helped) then there is a good argument to be heard that my acting was not a success.

I could have spent those funds on charities that I believe in. My wife and I love to give, but there would have been more to give had I acted differently. I could have spent that time continuing to build the two businesses that have given me the platform to share my material. I spend time there, but there would have been more time had I acted differently.

My own recent decisions paints the picture clearly that there is a good reason there is little self-management material. A self-management resource would, by definition, have to tell us how to limit, or control ourselves.

That scares us!

Freedom is the one virtue that is upheld across political parties in the US. Freedom is exalted as the one ethic that needs no explanation. Robert Bellah writes in *Habits of the Heart*, "Freedom is perhaps the most resonant, deeply held American value."[38] Bellah was a UC Berkeley sociologist and Habits of the Heart is a widely discussed work. He says that the emphasis on freedom has resulted in American's respect for individuals. A high view of freedom leads to tolerance in a diverse society as well as resistance to tyranny.

That is why, in my assessment, there is little self-leadership material in the American market. We know people will buy, "tell others how to act". We will spend our money on a systematic way to multiply our influence because when others do as I say, there is more freedom for me. I will have more time and resources to do the things I want to do if I learn to get others to act in the direction I lead them.

However, buying a way to control myself, rather than free myself sounds stifling. We know we need it, but it just doesn't have the same ring as Leadership.

But also hear Bellah's warning. "The ideal of freedom makes Americans nostalgic for their past, but provides few resources for talking about their collective future." He is showing us that romanticizing freedom can result in an inability to confront one another. We need to be able to confront one another, but definitely ourselves. Self leadership is being able to confront your impulses and act differently. The lack of material is because the concept is tough to think through and tougher to sell.

However, check those leadership books one more time and you always find the phrase, "You can't learn to lead others until you learn to lead yourself".

I wrote *Last to Least*, not because I think it is sellable, but because I believe it is helpful.

It is the prequel to every leadership book....ever.

If limiting yourself scares you, I understand. But remember this. I am talking about the kind of limiting that is most freeing. A bat is limited by light, true, but that is what makes the Dark Knight such an amazing hero.

My friend Turkey was limited in his patience with high school students, but he has unlimited patience when he is molding clay. He had to make a tough decision with his work. He left a safe career that he spent years and money to achieve to create characters with molding clay for people to enjoy. He was not sure if limiting himself to a startup without benefits was a great idea, but he decided his work was in creating art. Thankfully for so many people who enjoy his work, he limited his comfort and it was freeing. There were multiple outcomes, but in every choice, there were X's and Y's that could not be simultaneously acted out.

Last to Least is an approach to managing ourselves, so we find freedom to maximize our production!

We have focused on being neighbors-guided in our daily actions, but this neighbors-guided approach can help us make decisions when changing careers as well.

Turkey did not leave teaching school until his market proved to him that he was meeting their needs. They did so by purchasing his product. If I take a neighbors-guided approach to starting a new career or starting a small business I can ask a quantitative and a qualitative question.

"Will I be able to meet needs more fully when I take this step?

"Will I be able to meet more needs after I make this step?"

If you believe the answer is yes, but the start up fails or you do not get the position, then you have two options.

Option one, you may not be equipped to meet the needs you think you are. This is not mean. In my years chasing music dreams I met many people who thought they had the gift of singing. The problem was, no one had the gift of listening to them. You will have to believe in your abilities when no one else does to be successful at meeting needs. However, when ample time has passed and nobody has benefited from your work, then accept that you need to be better prepared or educated or let it redirect your career to something else that you may not even know you are good at. Unplanned opportunities is sometimes the only way we find what we are good at.

I sat down in the home of former Governor of Georgia, Nathan Deal. You could hardly argue with the success of one of the 50 governors of the United States. He said, "I never mapped out becoming Governor of Georgia. I tried to do the best job of serving the people that trusted me and focused on developing myself and my character over my position". That is not advice you hear in the self help world right now. Most say, "do what makes you money" or "do what you love". It is driving me crazy how much is being promised if people will "do what they love." But listen to someone who had incredible political and personal success. Nathan Deal was not looking for a title or position, he was looking to meet needs and become a person of character. Yes, he fought to win elections, but that was not his guide, the needs of those he served were.

If you find yourself not moving "forward", be able to admit that you need to develop the prequel to leadership. Develop your abilities. Develop a systematic way to lead yourself or adopt one like *Last to Least*. If you are not meeting needs, but you're ok with that because you are "following your passions" then at least do not call it work. It is not, no matter who tells you differently.

Option two, admit that you were not fully meeting needs and slowly change your process. If you are convinced you are in the right career or business, this is your path.

Ken Blanchard talks about this in Raving Fans. He says we should define our own vision of what we offer and be clear about what we do not. That is when we are answering yes to one of the previous questions. Kevin said, "Yes. I can meet people's need to enjoy their coffee in a creative zombie mug better than meet a high schoolers need for education."

Blanchard says next we should listen to our customers vision for what we should provide. That feedback can come in many ways. Sometimes Kevin hears, "You should make more mugs", but he chooses to spend the extra detail time it takes to make each mug unique and valuable. He has heard, "you should make some mugs other than zombies". He adjusted his actions when he heard this comment and began making other types.

This brings us to Blanchard's third point. Deliver your initial vision plus one percent. Kevin continued to deliver his initial vision that met needs. He made high quality zombie mugs. Then as he heard customers express other needs, instead of trying to meet them all, he changed one percent at a time. He began offering other characters besides zombies. If he tried to deliver on customer desires to offer other mugs AND offer more mugs at the same time, it could have ruined his business. He chose to make small changes as he allowed the needs of his neighbors to guide his work.

Kevin and Ken Blanchard and Nathan Deal have all realized that leading themselves in a neighbors guided way was the necessary prerequisite to leadership. You may have a title and not be confident in your leadership. It may be because you skipped this prerequisite. Let *Last to Least* be your prequel to your leadership story, filling in the gaps you are missing. You may be an aspiring leader looking for a platform. Make sure you write this prequel to your story before the leadership story begins. You may not share the prequel with others until later, but it must be present if you want to be the leader you can be!

PART 6

WHAT IS *LAST TO LEAST*? (CORE TRAITS)

We will never change the way we act until we change the way we think. The following are core traits that are so essential to *Last to Least* they are not simply what we "do". They are character traits of the system itself.

FULFILLING PROMISES BEFORE PURSUING DREAMS

Dreams are incredible! At every stage of my life I have loved to daydream about the things that could happen in the future with respect to the current job I was doing. When I was working to get into medical school, I thought about how comfortable my life would be and how I would be respected in the community. When I was writing songs, I thought about the artist who would sing them or the award speech I would give. When I worked in banking for a short time, I thought about moving up the ladder and leading a region for my company!

When I came into insurance, I wanted to set records. In my initial interview, I was asked how many policies I thought I would sell, and I answered immediately. My interviewer was a little startled and asked how I had come up with that exact number. "It is one more than the most my manager told me he had ever sold," I said.

I am not thrilled to tell you about my young arrogance. but I always see the BIG things which could happen. I am always looking ahead to how I may change the landscape of my industry. Following your dreams or setting loft goals is not inherently bad. However, you cannot forget to fulfill the promises you made before you set off to pursue your own ends.

While I was writing this chapter, I decided to stay after work one Wednesday night. Earlier, over lunch, my wife and I discussed that the class I taught at church on Wednesday evenings was over, but she and the girls still had one more week before we all took a break from Wednesday night meetings for the upcoming holidays. She smiled and said, "I bet you are happy to get to spend some time alone tonight."

I could not hide it! I was really excited to continue to flesh out the ideas which had been coming together in my mind around this very book. When I got back to work, I was so excited I started pulling up the document to write down some ideas. The phone rang. It was a client needing a simple change to their policy. I felt something inside me wanting to put the client off so I could go ahead and work on my book. I then felt the heat of the irony of the situation.

I was writing a book about putting aside myself to make sure others needs are taken care of, but I was unwilling to put my dreams of presenting my ideas to the side and help the person on the phone who I had promised to serve when I took their premium payment. A few minutes later, I got a text from my pastor. He said he was sick and unable to lead his class that same night and wanted to know if I could fill in. I again felt the same heat! I am on staff as part-time worship leader at the church and I am promising to help when needed. He would not have been upset if I said I could not, but the truth was I could.

I have never made a promise to write a book, but I have made a promise to serve people who pay me premiums and to be available when needed at my church. I was laughing with my wife on the way to church as I said, "How could I turn down filling in tonight to write a book about making yourself least important in a work equation?"

I think this thought pattern is common because of the value we have on new and creative ideas as well as our tendency to be looking for the next BIG thing. Americans only stay in jobs 4.6 years on average, so we are looking to jump ship when something we perceive as better comes along.

Last to Least is putting our promises and commitment first, before pursuing a new or better option. We should be as concerned with taking care of today's clients who have already paid for services as tomorrow's prospects who bring in new revenue. *Last to Least* is hiring extra staff to fulfill the timely service of current clients instead of letting them suffer as we pursue new clients.

RECOGNIZE THE DIFFERENCE BETWEEN WATERING VS. GROWING

To be a leader, you must influence others. To lead yourself, you must admit that the actions of others are ultimately their choice. There is no contradiction between the last two sentences. Even at gunpoint, you or someone you are seeking to influencing has a choice. Sometimes the choice is simple. Be shot or hand over $5, easy choice. Be shot or hand over my child, easy choice in the opposite direction. Be shot or hand over some other example between those two extremes maybe not so easy a choice. As a leader, you can decide consequences, but as a self-leader you must see the difference between your unilateral actions and the bilateral cooperation of others you seek to influence. Unilateral actions are those you can do without the cooperation of anyone else. Bilateral cooperation is when someone else has to act also. This applies to those I am asking to buy a product, to those I am trying to inspire to respond to my leadership, and to those with whom I am seeking to build a relationship. In each of these areas, I will be constantly frustrated with the lack of motion toward "growth." In these moments of frustration, I can manage myself well if I measure my unilateral actions instead of only the bilateral results I hope to see. Let me make it clear what I mean by unilateral or bilateral.

I pulled my three girls in close a few mornings ago. I told them I liked to write thank you notes to people who have impacted me, but "Since you two littles can't read, I am going to just tell you my note." I thanked them and told them how happy it made me that they were my best friends. They do not understand the word "relationship," so I just used the word friends. I explained that I tried my best to make friends with people, but that sometimes, no matter what I tried, there was not return of friendly action. I have never expected them to pursue me first, but to have a relationship, there has to be response from them after the relationship is initiated. I told them how happy it made me that they reacted to me being friendly and were friendly back.

On the way to school that morning Livie said, "Daddy, everybody's plant at school is growing leaves except mine. You can see their roots at the bottom of the cup but not mine." I could not believe what a perfect illustration for what I had thanked them for earlier.

"Did you water the plant?" I asked

She said yes.

"Did you put it in the sunlight?"

Yes again. "And I gave it plenty of room to grow!"

"Did you do everything your teacher asked you to do?" I asked one more question and the answer was yes again.

I told my daughter (while really reminding myself) that there was a wise person who once said, "I planted, my friend watered, but we are not in control of the increase." In sales, farming, education, or even building relationships, we will become frustrated or disillusioned if we are managing ourselves under the assumption that we can guarantee the increase of fruit. The point is, we can do the work of watering and not produce fruit—and that might be ok.

A few pages back, I discussed the importance of humility in the context of putting the needs of others above our own. The other side of humility is not thinking too highly of ourselves. You can see how one goes hand in hand with the other. Thinking more highly of ourselves than we ought can take many forms as pride often does. Thinking too highly of ourselves is easily seen when someone tells of their many achievements and brags about their contributions, but there are subtler forms.

I hate to admit it, but when I was thinking music may be a real career for me, I could hardly watch an award show without feeling sad. I even stopped watching them for a while. I would have told you at the time I was sad because I had tried to have a music career, and it just was not working out for me. According to my estimation, I was thinking of myself as a bad musician, and I needed some serious positive energy instead of reminders of my lack of success.

In reality, this was the more subtle form of thinking too highly of myself. I really thought I was a great musician and singer and songwriter, but I was not getting the recognition or break I deserved. Upon closer inspection later, I realized my sadness while watching the shows was coupled with a scorn for the award winners. I tried to squash it in my own mind, but every time someone went up, I would have some dismissing thought about their work. "His lyrics are corny," or, "She is tough to watch. Her movements are unauthentic." It really pains me to write this part, because I hate that I felt that way, and I hate when I am tempted to think that way now, but I hope my transparency about my negativity challenges you to examine your own.

When managing myself with me at the center, I am tempted to be critical of others who are receiving recognition for their work when I am not. I am thinking much too highly of myself when I feel this way, but sometimes the experience feels like I am thinking poorly of myself! "I am just not good enough," I may say, but I am really thinking, "I am good enough and no one can see it." Blatant or subtle, the fact remains—thinking too highly of myself leads me to frustration and envy because I am believing I have not received my due. I am actually having tension between the power I think I have to change my situation and the lack of the changes I see in my reality. Then, when the lack of power surfaces, I am angry with those who did not submit to my expectation.

Instead of thinking about how to do the small things a performer does each day to build a craft and network, I set my mind on the results that would come. I was in complete control of practicing and asking others to write songs with me, but I was not reminding myself that those were the things I could control, not who was given a Grammy.

If I am thinking too highly of myself , I will irrationally discount the success of others. If I am vocal with these criticisms, I am damaging my own reputation and credibility. If I am constantly belittling a high performing worker, can I really be counted on to see clearly the work I am entrusted to undertake?

Last to Least is realizing what you can control and what you cannot and then acting on what you can control. That alone can utterly squash envy and empower us to act at the same time! We are no longer focusing on others results, or our own results, but our own actions that can serve our neighbors. You are probably familiar with the prayer of Alcoholics Anonymous, commonly thought to have been written by Reinhold Niebuhr:[39]

> God, give me grace to accept with serenity
>
> the things that cannot be changed,
>
> Courage to change the things
>
> which should be changed,
>
> and the Wisdom to distinguish
>
> the one from the other.

I think it would be difficult to read that prayer and have anything but admiration for the author and a silent head nod in agreement— but we do not work this way. We have trouble with the wisdom to know the difference in what we can and cannot change. When we are trying to go worst to first, we only see the results. We start to focus on the results so hard we cannot see how powerless we are over how things turn out. If we succeed, we are anxious, because we are unsure if we can do it again. When we fail, we stop trying because we feel like our efforts are useless. If I did not think I could influence your thinking, I would have never written this book. I can present ideas and ask you to change your mind, but I am powerless to really change your mind.

My industry has the worst reputation for being results-driven, but others are not far behind. Sales companies continue to focus on the number of products sold as the nucleus around which every meeting and performance assessment revolves. I had a recent conversation with a friend who is a dentist. She was feeling uncomfortable at her practice because their weekly production meetings were focused on which dentist had produced the most revenue for the practice. She felt pressure to recommend more crowns and root canals as preventative when filling a cavity would have done the patient a better service. Even if some patients declined the offered services, my friend recommending them more often would lead to more revenue.

My friend felt tension between the focus of the meetings and her purpose as a dentist. She knew that if she could not determine the need of the patient she was seeing, she could simply make recommendations based on what she saw, and the patient could choose to accept or decline treatment. She knew she alone could not bring in one penny to the practice, but the patients had to accept her proper recommendations.

She could not promise more revenue if she saw people who did not need crowns, and I cannot promise sales if I meet people without needs. I know when I say that, you want to give me twenty examples of people who make sales when it seems like no one else can. I know these salespeople well, but when we promise to make a sale or bring in money, are we not thinking too highly of ourselves? When we bring all our attention onto the purchase of our good or service and put pressure on ourselves to deliver, we are failing to acknowledge what is utterly obvious. We cannot sell one thing without the cooperation of our customer. We cannot produce a new customer unless they walk in willingly. Oh, they can be convinced or coerced or even bribed, but we will have to admit the choice to part with their money is their own decision.

Why do we continue to focus on the thing we cannot control instead of what we can?

Last to Least does not think so highly of itself as to think it can control another person. Going *Last to Least* requires that I know the difference between watering the plant and growing the fruits. I must know the difference between the actions I can control directly and the results that come about because of decisions by someone else.

I have had this conversation with my pastor before. We talked about the mission of the church to "make disciples everywhere." A church may then set a goal to create 25 disciples this year. The Bible even tells the church how to go about this task. A pastor will tell you though, at the point of decision, he is powerless. He can tell someone how bad it will be if they do not surrender to their creator, or how great it will be if they do. Some evangelists may pull the hard sell, while others try the soft-touch method to convert unbelievers No matter their methods, all people who try to share the word of God believe themselves to be doing the Lord's work, However, they must all admit they cannot make the choice for someone else to become a "believer." When the moment of truth arrives, they are powerless to do the thing they are given as their central task.

If Dan Pink is correct and we are all selling something, then we have to admit we only have the power to influence, not compel action. We are powerless to make a child eat greens. We can discipline or even beat them, but we cannot make them eat. As my grandpa said, "I will make you wish you had done it!" That you can do, but you cannot make a child eat. That literally shocks some parents when I say it.

We are powerless to make someone take money from their pocket and buy a good or service, or eat healthier, or read an assignment, or talk openly with their spouse. If our work is intended to create these results it is wonderful, but a person who thinks *Last to Least* knows what we have power over and what we only think we do. I think we all know the only way to have measurable goals is accountability, but we have to think about the tension we create when we try to measure things outside our own control. In the example above about my pastor, he wants to see disciples made. That is, he wants to see people surrender to their creator instead of being the center of their own world.

Christians believe the way this happens it to hear the gospel of Jesus. The good news that God loves us, and he proved it by sending His Son Jesus to live the life we should have lived and die the death we deserve. The scriptures teach that believers in the gospel have been authorized to offer that same trade off with Jesus to others on God's behalf. The people in our church cannot make a decision for someone else, but they can present the story and ask someone to accept it as true. A great thing to measure, then, is not, "How many disciples did we make?" but, "How many times did we tell the story of Jesus and ask people to trust him?"

This idea has to begin to affect the way we monitor our own progress if we are going to be great self-managers. I have become thoroughly convinced the best way to monitor results is to see them as a temperature gauge instead of a goal. The results make us go back and evaluate the process, but the results should not determine if we feel our work was acceptable. I confess this takes thought to apply to each of our tasks and roles.

I know someone who was applying this model to his production in sales successfully but was having a hard time with some relationships within the company. His sales were at the top of the company, and he was using the *Last to Least* model to serve his clients well. But he also worked with some volunteers who were questioning some of his tactics, simply because they were different than his predecessor. One of his organizational roles is to maintain a "good relationship" with these volunteers. When he asked for advice from his executive leadership, they would tell him that part of his responsibility was to maintain a positive relationship with the volunteers, but they would never offer solid advice on how he should do it. It was causing tension in him because he was doing such a good job producing for the organization. However, it seemed like "maintaining a good relationship" with volunteers was just out of reach—no matter how he tried. When the executive leaders talked with him, he even asked, "What do you want me to do differently?"

They told him to "check his ego at the door" and to keep doing what he was doing but offer more explanation to the volunteers. He followed the advice, but nothing really changed. He was given the advice to buy meals for the volunteers and ask them questions about what they wanted to see happen in the organization but discount the advice they gave and continue working the same way. The Executives saw "checking ego" as equivalent to asking for advice that would never be used. The producer could not see it that way at all. It was a great position, but he even considered leaving the organization because of the unreasonable situation coming at him.

He was applying *Last to Least* to his sales, but he had been taught it was his responsibility to maintain the relationship with the volunteers. It was frustrating him to think he was failing. I was writing down his problem to try to advise him and I started thinking about his efforts to maintain positive relationships with the volunteers. I realized he is utterly powerless to accomplish this task alone. I wrote it down in his words, "to please the volunteers." I took a pencil and struck through the word "please" and wrote "appreciate." He realized he was utterly powerless to please anyone just as he was powerless to sell anything, so he had to stop thinking so highly of himself and admit what he could control. He could appreciate the volunteers on behalf of the company. He could thank them for their service. He could listen to their concerns, but he could not please them. The volunteers had a choice in how to interpret all his actions. The goal of "please the volunteers" is the same as "make a sale." Someone else is involved, and we have to admit when we are powerless.

I will continue to measure growth in my companies. All leaders expect growth from those we lead. However, if I do not know the difference between "watering" and "growing," I may completely misinterpret a problem in my organization. If I have a team member who is watering in every way I have prescribed, but there is still no growth, I may be tempted to doubt the team member's abilities.

In the example above where the sales professional was having a hard time maintaining good relationships with volunteers, imagine if I were his leader. If he was doing everything I asked him to do and was fully appreciating the volunteers, but they still did not respond, I may be tempted to think he was not cutting it. I may be tempted to believe someone else may do a better job if I look at the "growth" only. However, if I know the difference between watering and growing, I could ask some strategic questions. If he was watering the relationships, I would be able to know that the problem was not with him at all. I would continue to have expectations of a growth in the relationships or sales, or whatever I was looking for, but I would have better insight into the real problem.

As a leader, if my team is watering the way I have prescribed, but the results are not what I expected, I cannot blame them. I need to re-evaluate my own process and ask myself if I know the difference between watering and growing fruit.

There are barriers to our work in every direction. We know if we just had more capital, or more time, or less bureaucracy, or less competition, we could accomplish our dreams. There are things we can change and there are things we cannot change, no matter if we are able to see it or not. *Last to Least* allows us to see the situation more clearly, because we realize the difference between the two. We no longer measure things we cannot control, and we have courage to change the things we can for the good of the people we are working to serve.

FINDING MEANING IN THE WORK ITSELF

Barry Schwartz is the Dorwin P. Cartwright Professor Emeritus Psychology at Swarthmore College in Pennsylvania. In an interview discussing his book, *Why We Work*, Schwartz said some of the same words I have used to describe *Last to Least*, but I want to use his thoughts as a contrast to my message for clarification. As I have said, subtle changes seem small, but it may be the very breakthrough some of us need to make the impact we always dreamed of making, without the associated guilt of using others instead of serving others. Listen carefully to the distinction.

Schwartz first says the standard view is people work for pay, but he believes there are much more important reasons.[40] They want to do work which is engaging and challenging and "most important... they want to feel like somehow what they do makes somebody else's life better, even in some small way." That sounds a lot like what I am saying right? But listen closely to the subtle, but life-altering difference in the way he describes "make someone's life better" and *Last to Least* in the way we manage ourselves. He describes a group of janitors who were interviewed about their work. Most of them, he confessed, worked for pay, but a significant minority "worked for doing whatever was necessary to aid in pursuing the mission of the hospital." Still, we are tracking here with *Last to Least*. Then we take different routes.

He describes "doing whatever was necessary to aid in pursuing the mission of the hospital" as cheering up patients, making patients' families as comfortable as possible, and helping nurses turn big patients so they wouldn't get bed sores. "They were looking for ways to be helpful, NONE OF WHICH WERE PART OF THEIR JOB DESCRIPTION" (my emphasis added). These are truly "good" things these janitors were doing. The reason I want to make this distinction is when I talk about neighbors-guided work, this is exactly where people's minds go. Schwartz is giving an example of finding meaning WHILE you work, not IN your work.

Last to Least is neighbors-guided self-management in ALL THE TASKS ASSOCIATED WITH YOUR JOB DESCRIPTION. IF these janitors were to go through a learning session with me about *Last to Least*, they would have reported the same first sentence. They would say they "worked for doing whatever was necessary to aid in pursuing the mission of the hospital," but when they described what that meant, it would have been very different. They would have said they made families comfortable by giving them a clean place to rest and taking out the garbage so they would not feel cluttered. They would say they kept the halls clear of spills so doctors and nurses could get from room to room and efficiently treat patients. They would say they made sure the dirty sheets made it to the laundry so patients with bedsores would have clean sheets any time they needed. They would find meaning in performing the work of a janitor, not the work of a patient-care tech or a nurse.

Schwartz is saying people need to have meaning in their job, but describes finding that meaning outside their job description. What if we could learn to find meaning and purpose in the work we were hired to do, from janitor to CEO. You would not have to choose between meaning and job description. You could have both! I believe the entire workplace team would function to meet the needs of the community with greater productivity and efficiency.

What is *Last to Least*? Here's the recap. *Last to Least* is....

- Neighbors-guided self-management

- Self-sacrifice for the good of another

- Doing what I promise before what I aspire to do

- Accepting where you are powerless and measuring what you can influence

- Finding meaning IN your work, not WHILE you work

So, will you decide to go *Last to Least*? Will you make that choice to start considering the interests of those you are serving above your own? If you have read carefully, you realize this is not the kind of humility you are used to. This is not simply being nice. When we say treat others like you want to be treated, we think of being polite. *Last to Least* is so much more than being nice. It is an active search for needs that we can meet with our work. If you embrace it, your work will never be the same and you will not regret it!

PART 7

CULTIVATING YOUR IDENTITY

As I was walking through my 6-week *Last to Least* course face-to-face with a small business owner, he became convinced that neighbors-guided work was exactly what he needed to manage himself well. He was convinced that the answer to question #1 is "meeting needs" over any self-centered steering mechanism. He had come to this very section in the training and was ready to learn how to make the choice to go *Last to Least*. We recapped what we had learned, and then I reminded him of the three questions. I said, "The order matters as much as the questions." Then I gave him the questions again.

1. What is the guiding purpose of work?

2. Who achieves it?

3. How do they do it?

"That is what I need to know," he said, "How do they do it?"

I knew he would feel that way and maybe you do as well. That is why I keep saying "the order matters as much as the questions." Learning how to decide differently is as surprising as putting my neighbor first while I am least. This new direction for decision making, however, is what makes the choice to go *Last to Least*, last longer than a conference or a 6-week course.

Now we know what it is: *Last to Least* is a neighbors-guided system of self-management. If we are intrigued by this new way to work, we now have to choose to walk away from some of the past and toward who our work is designed to serve. I want to explore how to choose *Last to Least*. This will surprise you as much as when I told you work was not primarily about money.

CHOOSING FROM IDENTITY

When I began to research how we make decisions, I thought about my own experience in changing from worst to first to *Last to Least*. We all probably think a decision like this is based on a careful analysis of the facts. Others think of it in terms of emotional connection to the concepts. There are definitely some mind and some heart changes involved, but with such a comprehensive overhaul of the way we work, we need something more unshakeable and permanent.

James March is a professor emeritus at Stanford University. In his book, A Primer on Decision Making, he teaches us that people do not make decisions rationally or emotionally only, but according to their identity. A rational decision explores the cost-benefit analysis. When the reasons for a "yes" outweigh the reasons for "no," we say yes. His research revealed that we actually make decisions against that analysis every day. We make irrational decisions. These decisions, he found, are not based on the question, "Which is best?" but rather based on the question, "What does someone like me do?"[41]

We know that many decision makers tell us to "go with your gut."

This type of decision-making rests on our feelings and intuition. As you may see, there is overlap of intellect and emotion and will in making a decision about how to manage ourselves at work. Decisions from identity, though, is a comprehensive way that will create a ballast for the many complex situations we face in our work.

March says our identity—who we tell ourselves we are—is often the foundation for our decisions. I think we can see his point if we examine what often occurs when people make decisions. Take a thief, for example, who decides he is going to stop taking things from others. If he came to this decision rationally it may look like this: "If I continue to steal, I am eventually going to be caught, so today I am not going to take this item." On the other hand, if he was deciding on identity, he may think, "I am a good citizen, I am better than this, so I am not going to take this item."

The first is from rational and the second from identity. To clarify further, making decisions from identity is not "good" character, rather, it is simply a way to make decisions guided by character, good or bad. You could also make poor character decisions from identity. If a young man is accidentally bumped in the subway, he may decide to retaliate against the other pedestrian. He could make this decision rationally or by identity. Rationally, he may say to himself, "Does that person deserve my retaliation? Will I get in trouble if I retaliate? Did this hurt me enough to cause pain to this person?". Or he could decide to retaliate according to identity, thinking, "Accident or not, nobody bumps me!" Do you see? He is saying that nobody like himself would allow themselves to be treated this way.

Whether good choices or poor choices, we make some decisions from rational, cost-benefit analysis, but many from identity. We make thousands of decisions every day. We decide how to pitch ideas, how to respond to objections, how to greet others, and how to enter a room. All these small decisions add up to tell the story of who we are and who we are determines if we work with ourselves in the center or our neighbor in the center. If we are going to choose *Last to Least* in the largest and smallest details, we cannot simply make a list of all the neighbors-guided decisions we must make. That would be utterly impossible. So, we must take the surprising, yet overwhelmingly effective indirect approach. With March's research in mind, we must change our very identity and that will change all our decisions!

I said from the beginning, *Last to Least* is not just creating new habits, but becoming a different person. Identity is the thread of consistency in us no matter what role we are performing, so building the identity of *Last to Least* will give us a common thread for our multifaceted work.

Sales Agents often come into my office and give me a scenario of how they presented a client with a solution to their needs and the client had an objection. My agents ask, "What should I say to these clients?" I have begun to say every time I am asked a similar question, "What would someone who was really trying to help them say?" See? I want the agent to see themselves differently, not just be able to win a verbal chess game with the client. I want the agent to see himself as the kind of person that meets need.

When we meet needs AND "win" in the form of money, recognition, and approval, choosing a neighbors-guided approach is simple. *Last to Least* is still meeting the need when we cannot see the direct connection because we have come to believe steering ourselves this way is better. Better is not always glamorous.

This is for those who know, while it is not as glamorous a story, choosing to stay at home with your children to invest in their lives is as agonizing and heroic as choosing to stay late hours and to climb from secretary to CEO. This is for physicians and nurses who perform a miracle surgery saving a life, but also for those who monitor blood pressure and cholesterol medications saving lives over decades. It is for teachers who turn around troubled students, but also for principals who work at the school whose graduates fill the labor force year after year. The glamorous outliers are the stories that we want to hear, but there are so many unnoticed sacrifices that make the amazing stories possible. What I have learned is that so many of the glamorous stories begin with someone who simply set out to meet needs. *Last to Least* can mean giving up power to someone more qualified or fighting hard to make sure you get influence over someone who would keep your work from serving your neighbor.

If all these small and large decisions are coming from our identity, then we need to know what makes up identity. Identity is essentially the character traits which define a person. What character traits we can anchor ourselves to so neighbors-guided work is achieved?

QUESTION #2: WHO ACHIEVES NEIGHBORS-GUIDED WORK?

The order of the three questions is as important as the questions themselves when managing ourselves with this upside-down system. We spent a significant amount of time addressing question #1, "What is the guiding purpose of work?" way back at the beginning of the book. Now you can see why. The first thing we want to do when we see a new concept is to ask, "How do we do it?". However, James March is helping us see that we make a significant amount of daily decisions about how to manage ourselves based on our identity.

We must ask, "Who achieves *neighbors-guided* work?" before we ask, "How they do it?". If we skip this question, we will be like so many who attend a conference or listen to a motivational speaker. We walk away excited, but soon the excitement fades and we are right back to making decisions the same way we always have. We have all experienced this before.

Why?

Because we try to rationalize decision after decision based on the new tactics, but when our guard is down, we make decisions based on our identity. When we come across 1000 other decisions that were not addressed specifically at the event, we go to identity. At the event we attended, we may have obtained some helpful information or clear action steps, but our identity never changed, so we go back to making decisions from identity and they are the same old decisions.

If we are ever going to see lasting change and go from *Last to Least*, we must form a new identity that can withstand the nuances and pressures of an ever-changing work environment. Peter Drucker told us we had to learn to manage ourselves as knowledge workers. To be able to achieve a new approach to self-management, we cannot simply change our actions.

We must change who we are at the core!

We must build a new identity.

Think about this story to help us see how new character comes before new actions.

There was a man who parked on the side of I-285 in Atlanta with a flat tire. A car pulled up behind him, and the occupants of the car not only fixed the man's tire, they beat him severely and stole his car. As the man lay in his own blood on the side of the highway, a religious leader drove by. Traffic stalled so the leader had to look at the traveler, but no help was given. Next an activist drove by with signs spilling from the car demanding change. Traffic stalled so the traveler had to be seen, but there was no help given. Last an imam passed by on the way to the mosque. The imam drove the traveler to a hotel and offered the manager his credit card for the traveler's stay until he was healthy again.

Who was a neighbor to the traveler?

Asking what I have to "do" to go *Last to Least* will not lead to any character change. When the imam in the story woke up, he could have never foreseen his encounter with the traveler. He had to build the character traits required to stop and help long before that day. He was a neighbor to the one in need. I want to meet the imam, and I want to learn what makes him the kind of person who would take a risk and time to help someone in need. I want my work to look like that.

THREE E'S OF CHARACTER TRAIT DEVELOPMENT

With James March's research in mind, let's do what we have been doing the entire journey from *Last to Least*: let's find better questions. Instead of asking what to do, let's ask, "What kind of people go *Last to Least*?" And since character traits are the building blocks of an unshakable identity, we could ask more specifically, "What character traits do we need to develop to go *Last to Least*?".

When we are purposefully developing new character traits, three E's will guide us.

First, we need the traits EXPLAINED to see that we need them.

Then, in each section, I want to provide some inspiration to develop the characteristics we are trying to achieve. We need an EXAMPLE. Simply thinking, "I want to persevere," or, "I wish I was more patient," is not usually enough to develop these traits. When we are provided with the right inspiration for these traits though, we are often moved to imitate what we have seen in others. I hope you let these inspiring stories propel you toward becoming the person your neighbor needs!

Third, in each section, we need a reminder of when we EXPERIENCED the trait. When has someone displayed the traits FOR YOU? As powerful as it is to see them in someone else, it is even more powerful to motivate action when we remember these traits have been employed for our own good. Experiencing these traits is when someone displayed them for your personal gain or well-being.

Think about the power in this.

Imagine I received a personal loan from someone who believed in my start-up business. Let's say they loaned me $500 million. Imagine I began to see that my business plan did not account for all variables, and I was going to lose the investment. I may go to the lender and ask for leniency. Imagine if the lender said, "I am going to forgive the debt you owe." There is no way I could have repaid the loan, so you can imagine the gratitude I would feel toward the mercy of the lender. But how would you feel if you heard the following week I took someone to court over a matter of $100? If they could not pay, and I had them taken to jail for the amount they owed, you would find me repulsive. That is what these stories are meant to help us see. How could we turn around and be short tempered with so many others when we ask for understanding when we mess up? How could we demand accountability with no mercy to those who wrong us, when we ask for understanding about our own haunted past and mistakes?

Hearing the stories of those who have displayed these traits for me will hopefully remind you of your own examples. As you remember, I would encourage you to jot them down somewhere for the days when you are tempted to tether back to money or approval. Identity is made up of character traits, so we will use these traits as the building blocks of an identity that will not easily be lured to cut ties from our neighbors needs in exchange for self-centered motives. You will notice the pattern of this section. This pattern is the The Three E's of Character Development:

1. Character Trait Described (Explained)

2. Inspirational Example Seen (Example)

3. Inspirational Example Experienced (Experienced)

SELF-CONTROL EXPLAINED

If *Last to Least* is a system of self-management, then self-control is an obvious character trait necessary to this neighbors-guided approach. You can do a quick search of quotes about self-control and find it has been a topic of conversation since the beginning of recorded history. We could plumb the depths of the most brilliant quotes, but sometimes wisdom is found in the simplest places. With three daughters and movie players in our cars, the quotes I hear most often are from Disney movies. I have not "seen" many of these movies, but I can quote almost every line from *Moana* and *Frozen* and lately, *Mary Poppins*—my wife went a little retro and the kids loved it!

Frozen[42] in particular is a movie that perfectly captured the tone of our view of freedom. We cannot really talk about self-control without talking about freedom. Look at the way freedom and self-control come into play in *Frozen*.

Elsa has the power to create snow and ice. When she accidentally hurts her sister with the power, her parents try to teach her to conceal it. When told the power will grow, her father says, "She can learn to control it, I am sure of it." She has a more difficult time concealing the power when angry or nervous. "Conceal, don't feel," they say. She is taught to manage herself by not feeling the emotions, and therefore the powers are suppressed. When the powers come out in a highly stressed moment, she leaves town. In a moment declaring her freedom, she decides to "Let it Go." She enjoys her powers and makes a beautiful ice castle away from everyone she felt she had to hide from. In the song she sings, "No right, no wrong, no rules for me. I'm free!"

In Elsa's mind, and in the minds of many Americans, freedom is the absence of rules. She sees when there are no rules for her, she is free to follow any impulse she desires. This is the libertarian model of politics. Do whatever you want as long as it does not hurt anyone or impose on someone else's freedom.

But David Foster Wallace, who I quoted in the introduction, says that there is a problem with this way of thinking about freedom.

> American economic and cultural systems that work very well in terms of selling people products and keeping the economy thriving do not work as well when it comes to educating children or helping us help each other know how to live—and, to be happy, if that word means

anything. Clearly it means something different from whatever I want to do—I want to take this cup and throw it right now, I have every right to, I should! We see it with children—that's not happiness. That feeling of having to obey every impulse and gratify every desire seems to me to be a strange kind of slavery. Nobody talks about it as such, though. We talk about the freedom of choice and you have the right to have things and spend this much money and you can have this stuff. Again, saying it this way, it sounds to me very crude and very simple.[6]

It is hard to refute this logic when you see what kind of damaging addictions form when people follow their impulses. There is often nothing resembling "happiness" or "life" at the end of choices led by impulse. It is a child's desire that makes him follow a kidnapper back to his van for a promised treat. When we follow these desires it is inevitable that they keep us trapped where we no longer want to be. It is also not just the Freudian Id versus Superego battle we are seeing here. Freud believed we had to balance between the part of our personality driven by impulses toward pleasure and desire or the "id," and societal pressures or a sense of right and wrong, called the "superego." He said our "ego" was what balanced between the two. But as David Foster Wallace insightfully points out, we become enslaved by our impulses, not just outside pressures.

Elsa thought it was a form of oppression to be controlled by the views of others, but David Foster Wallace is saying it is oppressing and simple and childish to have to obey every impulse. Where are we to turn?

My brother and I started Ryals Brothers because we saw an opportunity in the market and our combined experiences prepared us to meet the needs of our neighbors. I have mentioned it already, but Ryals Brothers is our trucking and grading company that has seen exponential growth in just 3 years. 10X is awesome for any company, but businesses that start from scratch have a tiny survival rate, yet we attribute so much of our success to developing self-control and a neighbors-guided approach. We bought a few dump trucks and started hauling asphalt, dirt, gravel, etc. I created a logo for the company with the head of a donkey in the center and sent it out to the family... My mom texted me and said it was a perfect fit for two asses. I couldn't agree more. The donkey has been a trusted beast of burden for centuries. People have trusted the donkey to move their loads and take stress off their own backs. That is exactly what we wanted to do. When the donkey was accepting a new load, the owners would put a yoke on the donkey. The yoke was designed to be attached to the wagon, and the donkey would use her strength to pull the load.

Freedom and self-control are about choosing our yokes.

If I want to have the freedom of retirement, then I have to put on the yoke of saving. I choose to control myself from spending, so I can use those resources later in life. If I want to be free to live a long and healthy life, then I put on the yoke of exercise, and I limit my intake of foods that are bad for me.

Every moment we choose some things to yoke ourselves to and other things to break free from. When we were creating a budget, I joked with my wife that we cannot say yes to everything. We have limited time and resources, and we are yoking ourselves to people and impulses and societal pressures every day. Self-control means we are committing ourselves to the yokes consistent with the purpose of our work. *Last to Least* becomes extremely important here.

I was talking with someone recently, who was preparing for a speech inviting people to sign up for a self-development program. She was nervous, so I asked, "What is making you anxious?" She said she wanted to look like she was prepared. She knows I am serious about MY needs and therefore MY fears the least important factor in my approach to work, so she then confessed that "looking prepared" was not a great reason to be nervous. I agreed heartily.

"So why should you want to do a great job?" I asked.

Then she put the audience members in the sentence, but still not as the guide. "I want them to think I am prepared."

I was rather blunt. "So, this is really all about you?"

"What do you mean?" she asked.

The problem was that she was not worried about giving a speech that would meet the needs of the audience. She just wanted to appear to be prepared for her own pride. In her mind, she was still not the least important among the attendees. This is so common when I am talking this through with people. It seems so simple, but we are all so drawn to self-centeredness, it is hard to practice it when we are preparing or doing our work. "The reason you should want to be prepared is because of Haley," I told her.

Haley was a member of the audience we both knew would be there. The reason she should prepare and deliver a great speech is because if she communicates well, Haley will walk back and sign up for something that will change her life! The speaker is now yoking herself to Haley. She was preparing, learning, practicing, and managing herself with the needs of Haley in mind constantly. There was still pressure to perform, but it calmed her to remove herself from the center because her true purpose was not looking good, it was convincing Haley. Haley became her focus, so when he stood on the stage, there was no room for self-doubt or self-consciousness.

Marketing 101 is "know your customer". That is why we are told to think of a target market and not just broadly approach everyone with a product. Knowing your customer now helps to manage the decisions you make about advertisements. You are still making the decisions, that is why the character trait is called, Self-control. That is why *Last to Least* is a neighbors-guided system of SELF-management. We are making the decisions, but we are not just going on impulses and yoking ourselves to our own gratifying desires. We are voluntarily submitting ourselves to the needs of those individuals and communities our work is here to serve.

The kind of person who is characterized by self-control is someone who will be able to go *Last to Least*. If we want to work with this kind of impact and productivity for our neighbor, then we need to develop self-control as part of who we are. Then we will not be led away to slavery by our own passions or dreams. Self-control is the most obvious trait we will need in order to manage ourselves. A large section of the population will say you are thinking too much if you begin to manage yourself. It takes thinking to overcome simply following your natural impulses and desires and beginning to tell yourself what to do. Someone said it like this, "Stop listening to yourself and start preaching to yourself".

SELF-CONTROL EXAMPLE

The book *Just Mercy* by lawyer Bryan Stevenson has gripped the hearts of readers worldwide and opened our eyes to injustices that are unfathomable in our "civilized" societies. I was shocked to learn about so many of the true stories of abuse of power and neglect of those who could not afford help.[43] He concluded the book saying that in America it is better to be rich and guilty than poor and innocent. His beating of the drum of injustice makes me want to get in the line and follow!

Injustice often has a power element and the weaker party can be abused by one which is stronger. It makes it especially difficult to have self-control when you are being overpowered. It is even more difficult to have self-control when someone is exerting their power and you have to suppress your own power for a greater reason. That is exactly what happened to Bryan Stevenson. In Chapter 10 of his book, he tells about going to meet with a client in a prison. As he enters the building, he passes a truck with a Confederate flag and bumper stickers with racially-charged messages. He reminds readers about the use of fear to control blacks in the south with lynching and threats. He asked to see his client, but the tall, white guard tells him he will have to endure a strip search to enter the jail. Attorneys do not have to go through strip searches, but the guard insists. When he lets him through, the guard reminds Mr. Stevenson that the truck outside belongs to him. This kind of abuse and intimidation would cause anyone to lose focus, but Bryan Stevenson shows complete self-control. Why? Avery Jenkins.

Avery is the client Bryan is going to visit and Bryan had chosen to serve the needs of Avery Jenkins. In an intimidating situation, he displays such poise that inspires us all. Later in the story, after a few days in court, Bryan visits the same jail and meets an entirely different reaction from the guard. The guard was present in the courtroom, heard Bryan speak boldly for Avery Jenkins and fight for the justice which had formerly been denied. The guard was so moved by Stevenson's selfless help, he could no longer hate a man he respected. Stevenson not only was now justified, but he heroically won the heart of the guard in the process. Stevenson did not have to show that kind of self-control, but in doing so he met the needs of his client and changed the heart of the guard.

I hope we can see this amazing story and be inspired in the same way this guard was inspired. I hope we can see our work is not about always having to justify ourselves, but sometimes we will show great self-control so we can do what our work was designed to do. Stevenson knew demanding his own rights might deter his time and attention from doing what he was there to do—serve Avery Jenkins!

SELF-CONTROL EXPERIENCED

What if you were the guard in the story above? Imagine the impact Stevenson's self-control would have had on you! Imagine if you were Avery Jenkins and found out about Bryan's selfless act for you? The next time Avery or the guard has a moment when they can follow their own impulses or yoke themselves to their neighbors need, I bet they remember what Stephenson did for them. Is there a time someone has shown great self-control when serving you?

I grew up in a small community which was very passionate about our religious beliefs. I became very cautious around anyone who believed differently than me. Even if someone was telling me something correct, I would close my ears when it did not directly align with my beliefs. I did start to see some inconsistency in what I believed after being forced to hear different opinions in college. Without a clear grasp on truth, I was struggling to find what I believed about the big questions of life. Then I met Levi. He had earned a PhD in areas directly related to these massive questions about existence. I told him about my struggle to really put all of my thoughts together. He asked if I would like to meet together weekly and try to settle on a consistent worldview. I do not think he foresaw that we would still be meeting weekly two years later, but these two years helped me talk through and face every inconsistency in my belief system. I was able to see and accept all views had some existential problems to face. Our meetings helped me the most by allowing me to come to grips with when it is ok to say, "I don't know." The reason this time with him is such a help to me today in managing myself is not any discovery we made along the way, but the fact he showed great self-control during our meetings.

I have always loved a good debate, so when I see inconsistency in someone else, I could sink my teeth in and be rather ungracious. At worst, it was frustration on my part for being so inconsistent myself. At best, I was really trying to understand what was consistent in his beliefs. I do not remember him showing frustration with me once. As he pressed me to think about my own inconsistencies, I would attack back in frustration. He would answer me calmly and passionately, never angry or resentful. He was never demeaning and never flaunted his education or power. He just did his best to explain his own thoughts and help me walk through my own. How could I, as the recipient of this kind of self-control, turn around and expect immediate understanding in the people I lead, sell to, or serve?

GRIT EXPLAINED

When I went through the confrontation and realized working to go from worst to first was self-defeating and futile, I gave up on working for myself. I did not, however, have *Last to Least* to guide me, so I became unmotivated and discouraged. I had mistakenly decided working with less vigor was the answer instead of changing my trajectory.

Going *Last to Least* is not about working less or forgetting profits. It takes a tremendous amount of hard work to make sure the needs of our neighbors are met. It takes a tremendous amount of capital to see communities developed and barriers to be crossed. If you have breathed a sigh of relief to leave behind monitoring things out of our power because you think it will be easier, you are mistaken. It will be simpler, but that actually makes it more difficult. When we are trying to vaguely hit the goal of "sell one unit" or "have students who pass," we can hide behind the market or a hard-headed teen if we fail. However, if our systems of measurement become, "Ask 32 people for an appointment," or ,"Prepare for X hours each week before class," then the accountability piece falls to us, not someone else. If we can no longer pass the accountability we must be prepared to endure.

Grit is a character trait we need if we will ever meet the needs of our neighbors. Grit is courage and resolve, or as Angela Duckworth (more on her in a moment) puts it, "the power of passion and perseverance". I have seen how grit and going *Last to Least* build on one another in my own industry. Especially since Dan Pink has taught us that everyone is in sales and Peter Drucker taught that more and more knowledge workers are filling the workforce. These concepts are applicable across most work. Pink calls grit buoyancy, others call it fortitude or faithfulness.

Life insurance is a product most people agree is necessary in planning for our financial future. However, sometimes people I meet will tell me they do not have the money to purchase the coverage. If that person just insured a brand-new truck which was financed and has a mortgage on their home, it is irresponsible to their family as well as the finance companies to refuse to purchase life insurance. That is why we all agree how important life insurance is today. We have a culture where we obtain things now and pay for them later. If we cannot promise we will live to pay for the items, life insurance keeps our promise to pay.

My wife always laughs and says if she asked someone if they wanted to talk about their life insurance and they said, "No thanks", she would smile and say, "Call me if you need me." My wife would not show a lot of grit in that situation. When it comes to loving our beautiful daughters (or their Dad for that matter) you will see her show immeasurable grit.

Why do we stop so easily? So many agents tell me they do not continue the conversation because they do not want to annoy the other person. Is that really true? Or does the agent not want to be viewed as annoying? There is a huge difference. Grit will keep us moving when we put our fears of "looking annoying" aside and persevere to see a met need.

In case you thought *Last to Least* was for the unambitious, consider the work of Angela Duckworth. She realized people with grit identify their work as having purpose. Angela Duckworth has studied grit in a diverse group from spelling bee participants to West Point military graduates. In her book *Grit: The Power of Passion and Perseverance* there is an entire chapter devoted to purpose. She says those who describe their work as a calling rather than a job or career are much grittier. "Those fortunate people who do see their work as a calling...reliably say, 'My work makes the world a better place.'"[44]

She gives an example of a transit engineer in New York who says he realized he was helping move people where they needed to go and a physician who realized he was passionate about well-being through mindfulness. Whose well-being? His patients.

Do you see where these "grit paragons" as she describes them, focus their attention? They are committed to a calling focused on their neighbor. If we want to change our minds about our work and truly go *Last to Least*, one of the characteristics we will need to develop is grit.

The stakes of being gritty in talking with a client about life insurance are high. There are thousands of stories of agents who sold policies to families and when the bread winner died, it enabled them to continue to live well. Likewise, there are countless stories of when families, generations even, were changed forever because of untimely death without life insurance. IF the need is real, and I am considering the needs of my neighbors, then I will not stop asking when I get worried about looking annoying. I will forget myself and look to their interests. I see a need they do not see.

Of course, we all know there is a time to quit.

Even Angela Duckworth admits there are times when we can be too gritty. Our discomfort, however, is not a reason to abandon the unseen needs of the neighbor in my care! Worrying about them being annoyed rather than me looking annoying is the key to neighbors-guided work and results in a more accurate assessment of when to keep showing up and when to realize they do not want my help. If I am most important, I may stop asking too soon to avoid looking annoying. I may also ignore the fact my client does not need insurance. If I am least important and have developed grit, I will not give up too soon and I will not frustrate my clients by over-pursuing.

I will neither over-pursue nor under-pursue.

Chad is a 16-year agent in my office who had never qualified for a particular sales contest we have each year. In my first year managing this office, I realized he is not particularly motivated by more money or trophies. He had become interested in my *Last to Least* method and was enjoying working harder for his clients' needs. One problem he had consistently seen is that people hear him out, but then want to wait until a later time to buy. By that time, it is "out of sight, out of mind". I asked him one day if he ever mentioned his heart problem to his clients. "No", he explained, "I just feel weird trying to sell life insurance by trying to scare people." I agreed with him wholeheartedly. Scare tactics are not part of *Last to Least* and, frankly, they are becoming less and less effective in worst to first.

Chad's heart condition discovered at age 23 made him ineligible to purchase coverage. I asked Chad, "What if your brother wanted to wait a year to purchase life insurance and your nephew, who you love, was at risk?" I asked. "Wouldn't you remind your brother how you wish you could purchase life insurance today? What if some guy like you would have convinced your 22-year-old self to purchase coverage instead of waiting until it was too late?" I continued. "How would you feel about him?"

"I would be grateful for him," Chad said with a grin.

Chad confessed he would not tell his neighbor the same persuasive story that he would readily tell his brother. It took grit to ask people a couple extra times when they said they wanted to wait, and it also took going *Last to Least*. Chad has more integrity than any person I have ever worked with. When he added the development grit and found the new direction of working for needs, he became more productive than ever! Chad joined me as only one of ten agents in GA to qualify for the sales contest that year, and he has not looked back since.

Remember James March and his assertion that we base most decisions on identity rather than logic? If his claim is correct, and we do choose based on our identity, then to choose *Last to Least* we will have to develop the right characteristics, transforming not only how we work, but who we are. Grit is a character trait we need to improve upon if we are going to manage ourselves and place our neighbors at the center of our work.

GRIT EXAMPLE

Grit is showing up for our neighbor even when we are tired, afraid, confronted, or marginalized. The Civil Rights movement is full of inspiring examples of those who continued to show up so not only themselves, but their neighbors, could have a life of dignity and justice! Martin Luther King Jr. continued to lead people time and again even after being beaten or jailed for seeking justice! This excerpt from *Time* magazine makes it clear what kind of grit King possessed:

> As King told the story, the defining moment of his life came during the early days of the bus boycott. A threatening telephone call at midnight alarmed him: "Nigger, we are tired of you and your mess now. And if you aren't out of this town in three days, we're going to blow your brains out and blow up your house." Shaken, King went to the kitchen to pray. "I could hear an inner voice saying to me, 'Martin Luther, stand up for righteousness. Stand up for justice. Stand up for truth. And lo I will be

with you, even until the end of the world.'"[45]

On April 10, 1960 King spoke at Spellman College Founder's day about how to move mountains. He ended this powerful address by encouraging the students:

If you can't fly, run

If you can't run, walk

If you can't walk, crawl

But by all means keep moving![46]

His words are only surpassed in power by his life. As we know, he lost his life for the cause of justice. We cannot add to what he said with his life, but we can allow him to inspire us to move toward working for our neighbors with tenacity!

GRIT EXPERIENCED

My mother has always shown tremendous passion and perseverance when it comes to fighting for me. My mom has provided for our family for as long as I can remember. I remember many days when she was long gone before the rest of us woke up in the morning. She would work all day as a paraprofessional and then take care of and cook for four wild boys after that. She went into debt to finish her bachelor's degree in education to provide for us. Later, she obtained a master's and Specialist Degrees to optimize her ability to teach first grade students at Lula Elementary.

She could have used her earnings on her own indulgences, but the family needs were always held in higher regard. When we talked about higher education and the costs associated, she encouraged me to get scholarships and financial aid, but she always let me know that if I needed anything, she would move heaven and earth to get it. I took out loans to get through school, but I will never forget feeling homesick and calling my mom on a particular weekend. I did not have enough money in my account for gas. I am sure it was a hardship on the family, but after one call, there was money transferred to my account so I could get home. She kept getting up before everyone and kept sacrificing for me and the whole family even when I am sure there were days when she would have rather just given up.

There are times when it requires grit to keep going for my clients. Sometimes they do not show me the respect that I want or the gratitude that I believe is appropriate. At these times I should remember the grit my mother showed on my behalf. If she did that for me, how could I refuse it to someone else? I did not earn that kind of sacrifice from her, so how could I refuse it to someone who needs it?

Take a moment to think. Is there someone who has shown that kind of grit on your behalf? Let their goodness toward you be a motivator to display grit for those neighbors your work was created to serve.

This is a very personal and private example, but the trait of grit has also been exemplified for me in the public and corporate spheres. When I learned about the Civil Rights movement in school, I viewed it as something that happened in "history." I did not see the effects it had on the way we live today. I was actually taught that we should look at the "fairness" of opportunities that exist today instead of the history that lead to our current state. To oversimplify, my view was that all people had equal opportunity by law today, so that must be the way things actually worked.

Then I began to see what I cannot unsee. My friend's father, Sambo, could not have gone to the same high school as my father. That was not "history," that was very recent. I began to see the effects that years of discriminatory treatment could have even if the playing field was immediately "leveled."

For example, if I began to play Monopoly with you and every time you passed go, I punched you and then took your $200, I would have an obvious advantage. Assume we played that way for a couple hours. If we passed the same Monopoly game to our children, but my child said to yours, "That was unfair. You may keep your $200, but you can only buy property in the first section of the board." Assume they now played for a couple hours with the new rules then they handed the same game to our grandchildren. My grandchild said to yours, "That was unfair. Let's play with the original rules where I have no advantage." We would be foolish to assume all is "equal" now because there are no advantages "according to the rules."

In the example, you and I would represent slavery, our children Jim Crow days, and their children would represent laws that prohibited racial discrimination. An oversimplified example, but a powerful illustration of how current "equal" rules could still result in opportunities that are not as equal as we might believe.

When I allowed myself to see this reality, the Civil Rights movement and reconciliation efforts began to feel like they made a difference in my own life. I see the rich relationships I have personally as well as the cultural richness Americans (of which I am one) enjoy because of the efforts Dr. King made to end discrimination against people of color.

How can I stand by silently when I have been given so much? These new insights have created a burning desire to help others see what I once missed, to use my voice to speak for those who have been silenced. When I started to see Dr. King's grit go from something, I viewed to something I experienced, it began to change me and develop the same grit in me.

Will you look deeply into some of the private or corporate displays of grit to find where your life has been enhanced? Will you allow those experiences to move you toward showing grit for others in the very work you already do today?

GENTLENESS EXPLAINED

Gentle Dental is one of the best attempts I have seen to rebrand an industry often feared for perceived harsh treatment of patients. I ran across the website of Gentle Dental which touts, "The largest dental practice in the New England." Grinding, picking, filling, root canal, are not words that evoke images of a sommelier delicately presenting a bottle or a masseuse gracefully relieving stress and tension. No, the dentist is a fear for so many because the harshness of the metal to enamel and the sound of the whirring drill make some people uncomfortable just walking into the building.

With the name of the business, Gentle Dental, they are trying to change the perception before you even arrive. I noticed my dentist has even another tactic to help me accept some of the harshness with a little more tolerance. I did not notice the gesture the first few times, but when I finally did, I realized the assistant had been doing it all along. Every time my dentist would approach my face with a needle for numbing, the assistant would take out her air syringe and blow a steady stream of compressed air onto my opposite cheek while flexing and extending her elbow to move the air around my face. It was not just a distraction, but it served to help me receive the needed anesthesia with a more pleasant experience. Gentleness is a characteristic of those who will achieve *Last to Least*!

Gentle people know working with others or for the good of others often requires offering them what is best for them even though it is unpleasant. There are two ways to make that offer: with a rod or with love. There are also two ways to respond when the neighbor you are serving opposes you as you work with their needs and the needs of the community in mind: again, with a rod or with love. Gentleness is not being a pushover and gentleness is not always agreeing, but gentleness is focusing on the way your neighbor receives your services. To clarify further, gentleness is not focusing on what your neighbor thinks of you, but again, the way they receive your service.

If we are selling a product or service, educating a student, or prescribing a treatment we are constantly making offers. "Take this medicine twice daily for a week," or, "Do you feel comfortable with that price?" or, "Use the scientific method," are all offers we make to consumers, patients, and students. These offers are there to change the beliefs or behaviors of those we seek to influence. We want them to buy or take the medicine or use a different mental road map.

Neighbors-guided offers are much different than me-centered ones. Coercion is a tactic used to achieve the desired behavior from our customer, student or patient. A person using coercion is often managing themselves with ME in the center. I may believe scaring my neighbor into action will mean I have done my duty, or I will earn a commission, but the neighbor's needs are pushed to the periphery. There is no doubt making a request with a club in one hand while patting the end of the club with the other hand is an effective way to change behavior. However, this type of coercion does not promote community exchange of service, but makes neighbors withdraw their connection with one another.

The coercion test is a widely debated, but established metric created by the Supreme Court in the case of Lee v. Weisman.[47] The court ruled a student was being coerced by a principal if the principal invited a religious leader to pray at graduation. The court voted coercion was not just blatantly forcing a student to pray or not pray, but even the pressure of having to stand when others stood for the prayer was enough to be ruled as coercion. No matter what we believe about school prayer, this helps us see making offers with a rod does not always look like a bully with a bat. Would you rather be pressured into movement, or would you rather be persuaded? A gentle person knows how to appeal to a potential patient or client's desires, rather than to use force to cause a decision.

Dan Pink says the new ABC's of selling includes attunement.[48] He says we should not always be closing a product we need to sell, but to be tuning into the needs of the neighbors we serve. Sometimes this requires listening and getting underneath what our neighbor tells us they need. A member of my office staff recently told me we needed to hire another employee because of how busy we were while people were out to lunch.

I asked, "What is the real challenge here for you?"

She answered, "I think we just need another body around to help at that time".

"Isn't that a solution?" I asked. "What is the challenge that another person would help solve?"

When we talked through it together, I realized the problem was my employees thought I expected them to answer our neighbor's needs immediately when they called and did not want them to have to leave a message. I was able to put a better messaging system in place and clarify my expectation of "great service" and the problem was resolved.

Do you see that? Sometimes we are presented with problems that are not the real problem. We have to attune ourselves to the needs of those we serve, including our own team, if we are leaders. If I simply said, "We do not need another person, just get back to work or find another job," would my team member have been inspired to serve the needs of our neighbors?

We will not go unopposed when we are making our offers to serve others. There is constant disagreement and gathering of facts as people make decisions and we work for their good. A gentle person sees these as opportunities to clarify and help their neighbors see what they cannot see, not as times of frustration.

"You don't know my students/clients/patients" you may say. "They only respond to brute force." There is a time for force even with the gentleness. However, gentle people know that time comes slowly. Let those times be for the foreheads of stone. Some hard-headed people will oppose until the end. Sometimes a dose of reality is the only thing that will soften the exterior and allow them to accept needed advice. One example of these rare cases might be when a doctor needs to tell a stubborn patient they will die if they do not receive the treatment being administered. Even these weightier pleas can be delivered with breeze! When a gentle person sees a solution to their neighbors' problems, they do not immediately stop bringing it to light just because the neighbor fails to see it.

GENTLENESS EXAMPLE

There is a YouTube video of Penn Jillette speaking candidly about a Christian who approached him to try to tell him how to have a relationship with God.[49] Penn says he himself is not a Christian, but solemnly tells the camera that if a Christian truly believes in what the Bible says, he must really hate his neighbor if he does not go out and tell them about what will happen if the afterlife without a belief in Jesus. Penn says the Christian who approached him was saying things he did not agree with, but there was something about the Christian Penn believed was sincere. This must have been a gentle man.

He tried to change Penn's mind and did not, but still gained his respect. Penn even said if there is a bus coming and he tried to warn someone to get out of its way and they just stood in its path, there was a point at which you tackle the person in front of the bus. Penn saw the man who confronted him as someone trying to tackle him, but still had great respect for this man. I would love to congratulate this Christian, and Penn Jillette for that matter, for being able to appreciate the feeling behind the message of Jesus even though he disagreed. That kind of gentle person is someone I want taking care of me, and that is what I want to do for my neighbor!

GENTLENESS EXPERIENCED

"D-Wight" is the way I answer the phone when he calls. Dwight is about 40 years older than me, but our experiences in the same industry and a kindred spirit has kept us in touch since we met. Dwight is one of the first people I ever told that I had a vision bubbling to write a book and coach others to do neighbors-guided work. We both knew public speaking would be a central part of the vision. Dwight had been planting the seeds in my mind that this was the direction I should pursue for years, but he knew my skills and ideas needed more development.

I got anxious. I was ready to get started and since Dwight had been encouraging me, I had conversations with him about the future. I started telling Dwight I was ready and, honestly, was searching for him to tell me that I was ready. Dwight saw the potential, but again, knew development was needed. I am thankful that Dwight had become gentle!

If he would have told me that I was ready, I would have become frustrated because I was actually not ready. However, if he would have failed to deliver the news in a way that I could receive, it may have crushed the growing vision that was brewing in me. He needed to have a special blend of reality and encouragement or I may not have continued on this path at all.

He had been telling me for months, "You missed your calling. You need to be in the public speaking realm." Then when I got anxious to jump from my career, I asked him to go with me to an event where I would be speaking. He had heard me many times but realized how serious I had become about following this vision. He knew there were other steps that needed to happen before I was ready to make the leap, but I was unable to see it.

I will not recommend saying to a person in your life what Dwight said to me unless you have a cultivated relationship. The exact words are not what I am looking for, it is the concept of being gentle.

"I am not saying you are Andy Stanley," Dwight said with a chuckle, "I AM saying that people listen to what you have to say, and you have a knack for delivering messages in a way that people can relate to." Andy Stanley is a communicator that Dwight and I both respect and have had multiple conversations about. He is the pastor of a massive church near our hometown. Dwight was affirming the gifts he saw me demonstrating, but he was also letting me know what I needed to hear: it was not time to leave my day job.

Now that Dwight has done that for me, how can I refuse it to others? Within a trusted relationship, Dwight delivered encouragement as well as tough news that added value to my life. He did not shrink back from delivering the medicine I needed but delivered it with a gentle touch, equivalent to the dental assistant distracting me from the pain of the oral shot. He did not shrink back from telling me the truth but did it in a way that would make it receivable.

Dwight is gentle! My life is forever better because he is. I want to be that for someone. Consider someone who has given you bitter news, but you realized, or may be just now realizing, that the news was for your good. Thanking them would be appropriate. Emulating them would be transformative.

JOY EXPLAINED

When I talk to others in sales about the way I manage myself, they often want to hear the triumphant stories of persistent production. My wife, on the other hand, always reminds me to tell about the massive difference in my (and her) happiness. When you live or work closely with someone, you can see when they are just changing a few behaviors or if they are changing into a different kind of person. I actually asked her to make a video talking about it to help others see what a dramatic effect this new identity and purpose can have on us and those we love.

"Always fearful, always worried, you could not stop thinking about the next achievement," is the way she describes the past. I was not joyful in my work and therefore, not ready to meet the needs of my neighbor, I was letting my lack of joy turn my neighbor into a pawn to make me happy. I thought it was just common sense that if I worked harder and achieved, I would be happier.

"If I know everything about your external world, I can only predict 10 percent of your long-term happiness," is an astonishing statement made by Shawn Achor, a Harvard-trained researcher of positive psychology. He says most companies follow a model for success like this: If I work hard, I'll be more successful, and if I am more successful, I'll be happier. But, he declares, that is a broken way of thinking. "If you can raise someone's positivity in the moment, that gives them a happiness advantage." Even saying, "Your brain at positive is 31 percent more productive than your brain at negative, neutral, or stressed."[16]

At this point, many of us have heard about of the power of positive thinking. Is it really all that it is touted to be? If I were to ask you right now why you are happy, you would point to things about your external world to tell me why they make you happy.

"I have all I need," you might say.

"My family is healthy," another person may answer.

"My husband or wife loves me, and I can take on anything when I am loved." This statement shows us your happiness is wrapped up in another person.

All answers are common and, I believe, true on some level. Is what Shawn Achor is saying different than what those surveyed are saying? It seems like it on the surface.

"It's not necessarily the reality that shapes us, but the lens through which your brain views the world that shapes reality. If we can change the lens, not only can we change your happiness, we can change every single educational and business outcome at the same time," Achor says.

So does joy come from an external source, or from within? Someone who reports that their happiness comes from personal success could be viewing life through either lens. Two people, Sam and Bill, may both say they are unhappy "because they are not successful". Upon further examination, we may ask, "How do you know you are not successful?" Sam explains he was happy when he made more money, but now he is making less money and he is no longer successful. He is allowing his circumstance to determine his happiness. Bill, on the other hand, makes more money than ever and is hitting every target at work, but still reports being unsuccessful. Bill's lens is negative no matter what his circumstance. He is always moving the target of success "out past the cognitive horizon" as Achor says.[16]

With that in mind, think about the people surveyed above. Some of those who report happiness is because of a "healthy family" may fall apart and lose happiness if the family became ill. What if, however, you learned the respondent had a child with cystic fibrosis? Does that change the way you hear the response? I think it does. With this person, we learn she is deciding to have joy based on something much more than circumstance. She has changed the lens through which she sees cystic fibrosis and reports being thankful for a healthy family, despite the health condition her child has. This person has a character trait of joy, not just circumstantial happiness. If you ask people surface questions, they may not respond, "I have a deep-seated character trait that cannot be shaken by mere circumstances." No, they may just say they are successful or healthy.

If most people surveyed say the same thing, then how can you tell the difference between those who have the character trait of joy and who are merely allowing their circumstances to feed their joy?

JOY EXAMPLE

When the money is gone, or health goes downhill, those with the character trait of joy continue to report happiness while those who were counting the costs and benefits will lose their happiness. We have all heard the naysayers who don't believe that having a positive attitude has the power to change your life for the better. The tongue-in-cheek country song, "Buy Me a Boat" makes the subtle point that money really can buy us happiness. Country star Chris Janson sings, "I know everybody says money can't buy happiness......but it can buy me a boat."[50]

He is making the case that money can't buy happiness, but it can buy things that make you happy. And those who achieve those "happiness markers," we will call them, can argue with those of us who have not achieved them because they say we just do not understand. These high-joy reporters may attribute their joy to a perfect family or significant promotions and for others it is a boat. This is how many self-help authors sell today.

"If you just keep pushing to get where I am," they say, "you too can have happiness".

And we do not have a lot to argue about, because we do not have and will probably never have what they have. Some of us just look out the window and pine for the day we can achieve what they have. When trials come, however, and they will come for us all, the joy, or lack of it, is revealed. See that? Revealed, not caused. For so many of these high joy reporters, the joy is very temporary.

Don't you want the kind of joy that can withstand trials? Don't you want to keep that 31 percent higher productivity for the good of your neighbor, even when life seems weightier than normal? With joy, you can be the kind of person who can keep achieving neighbors-guided work even when the money does not always come in the quantity you expected, or the boat is still out of reach?

So, we need to develop this joy as a character trait. Something deeper, a lens that illuminates in the great times as well as the trying times. As we have said, when we are inspired by stories of joy in trials, we may be able to achieve this kind of joy! Shawn Achor says dopamine in our brain not only makes us happy, but it opens up the learning centers in our brain. I think this is a key to understanding joy in trials. To have the power to continue to have joy, we have to believe these trials are making us into more complete neighbors. This lens will allow us to become equipped to serve our neighbors in better ways because we have chosen to learn from trials.

At a conference I attended, I heard Christine Caine, the founder of the A21 campaign speak. At that point I had never heard of A21, which is a non-profit organization working to end human trafficking, forced slave labor, and sexual exploitation around the world. Cain talked about the pain she endured from her own experience as a sexual abuse survivor. "When you're first abused, you're filled with shame about what is happening to you. When it happens over a long period of time, you then begin to think it's happening because of who you are."[51]

Abuse is a trail none of us would choose. Even if you have never experienced abuse, you know the pain is lasting and deep if you have had a single conversation with someone who has. There are few trials that have the power to crush joy like physical and sexual abuse.

The mission statement of A21, "To end human trafficking everywhere, forever," was so powerful I immediately felt small hearing it. The passion in Cain's voice was powered by a deep-seated joy rooted in her character. She is serving some of the world's forgotten neighbors and doing so against some of the fiercest opposition. The trials she faced in her early years, as ridiculously difficult as they were, have become a teacher she now uses as fuel to drive her service for her neighbors around the world. She says, "I think sometimes people see someone like me and they think that to do what I do, I've been exempt from trials and pain and suffering. In reality, I think, 'Oh no, my past has prepared me for what I do.'"

It would be completely natural to view these difficult times as proof the world is hopeless. So many would view trials of this magnitude through that lens, but Christine Cain has chosen to see it a different way. She is showing us joy can be experienced even through trials, specifically if we allow them to teach us to walk our neighbors through their own pain. Christine Caine is a perfect example of someone who has developed joy as a character trait.

JOY EXPERIENCED

Is there a time someone who has given up their own joy for you?

Is there a time someone has become stressed, so you could have joy?

Let that inspire you to acquire joy as a character trait that defines you in good times and bad. I know I have been served by someone managing themselves with me at the center. I took a different position in my company and at the same time, my boss changed. He was new to his role as well. There were some completely untrue things being said about my management, and I was being doubted by people who did not yet know me well. It would have been easy for my new boss to distance himself from the situation, but on the night of the meeting to clear things up, he walked in and sat beside me. He did not have to be there, but he stepped in and spoke for me many times in an intense meeting. He put stress on himself and carried a load that, who knows, I may not have been able to overcome alone. I was being accused and he took the brunt of the accusations. We both had great joy when the air was clear, and everyone had a correct understanding of what was going on. That incident made me incredibly thankful for him and we will forever share a bond, but it also prepared me to do the same for my neighbor. How could I look at someone now being wrongly accused and not step in? I feel compelled to do for another what was done for me! The hope is for my joy and the person I step in for when we come out justified.

CS Lewis is an author I enjoy greatly, and he says it completes our joy to have someone join us in admiring something we have seen as valuable. If there is something going on in your organization that brings you joy, do not keep it private. We do not do that with our favorite restaurants or our favorite movies. We not only praise these things; we try to get others to join us in appreciating them. "Wasn't that delicious?" or "Wasn't that plot turn amazing?"

Lewis says it not only brings another joy when you tell them about the delicious restaurant, but the recommendation somehow completes your own joy. If we want to develop joy so we can meet the needs of our neighbor, we view the world through a more positive lens, but we should also help someone else see what we see. The next time you have a meeting you would normally call a waste of time, find just one thing you found helpful and tell another member of the meeting about it! If you catch someone doing neighbors-guided work around you, let them know you saw them and tell someone else what you observed. If one of your competitors has a great year and you know they have served the community, call her and let her know you see the impact she is making. If someone gets the promotion or award you thought was yours, make sure someone hears you congratulate them heartily! It will spread joy and complete yours! Don't lose out on that 31 percent extra productivity. Your neighbor needs it, and your community needs it! It will cause people to want to be involved with you and your business!

PART 8

THE FOLLOW-THROUGH

Last to Least can be like a flashlight to a dim path in that it can help your find your way when you are feeling lost. However, there are other times when the path forks and both directions seem to lead to the same destination. For example, half of the country thinks caring for the poor means more tax-funded programs for the less fortunate, while the other half thinks fewer taxes will lead to more jobs that allow the poor to care for themselves. Everyone would agree the solution is likely to be more complicated than simple. We are trying to focus on the needs of others, but sometimes we need more clear signposts to help us on our way.

James March actually addresses this in his research I have already quoted. We said that we were building a new identity and that would affect our choices. We said the building blocks of identity were character traits, but there is another building block of identity. March also says that choosing from identity involves pre-set rules we live by. He says these rules give us an identity that withstands the pressure when making a tough decision.[41]

Bryan Stevenson tells about the power of identity in his famous Ted Talk.[52] His example involves a rule that his grandmother gave him when he was young. She made him promise he would never drink alcohol. He says, "...and to this day I have never drank alcohol. I do not tell you that because I think it is virtuous, but to show you the power of identity." This rule to "never drink alcohol" has affected numerous decisions in his life. There could be hundreds of times when he could have rationally decided that drinking was better than abstaining. I am sure there are countless times he has worried that his refusing to drink at a party may make him seem like an outsider; or worried that others would see him as judgmental. It is at these times of possible temptation or weakness that the power of this pre-set rule overrules the rational decision of the moment.

The Proverbs are full of these pre-set rules to keep readers on a wise path. We may think these preset rules are too broad to have maximum impact, but there are times when following these simple rules can change hundreds of other outcomes. Even more, when there are multiple rules that are followed simultaneously, there are times a decision will be made because any other decision would break one of the rules. The rules, when chosen to be followed, can act as individual road signs that collectively lead us to our desired location. If neighbors-guided work is where we are going, then to go *Last to Least* we have to choose the rules that will keep us moving in the right direction.

When my brother and I first started Ryals Brothers, our logo had a picture of the most trustworthy hauler in history, the donkey. It reads "You don't need the stress. We'll take your load off." When creating the company, my brother and I saw a need in our community. People needed different construction materials hauled, and they were having a problem with drivers doing what they promised. What if we could relieve that stress, keep their construction job moving, and employ dependable drivers at the same time? But again, our only neighbor is not the construction industry and our drivers. Those trucks pass thousands of families every day who are our neighbors as well.

During the early days of our business, we had only one employee, Joe. Let's say I sent Joe out on the road after a crash course in *Last to Least*. If Joe is able to maintain his focus on all the people he is responsible to, I am certain he would get loads covered quickly while maintaining the safety of the families he is passing. On the other hand, a speed limit sign is a great reminder he is responsible to those families if his attention to his speed ever wavers. The speed-limit sign is like the rules we set for ourselves in our lives—they make decisions for us without having to think about them. Returning to Joe the driver, there will be days for him when the truck breaks down or the superintendent at the job site knows nothing and cares nothing about *Last to Least*. There will be days when Joe's back hurts from driving too much and days when we have asked him to do more than what is possible in a day. There will be times when Joe does not know what to do or does not remember he is committed to *Last to Least*. See, we need the guide of *Last to Least* because we cannot have speed limit signs at every small choice we have throughout the day. We need a way to manage ourselves through the complexities, but we also need speed limit signs and mile logs to keep us accountable. Joe would much rather fill his tank with the premium fuel of the good of his neighbor, but when he is running on fumes, he will need something to keep him moving toward his target. Because we have our own days where we turn inward and get lazy, or tired, or embarrassed, we need some rules to live by to keep us accountable to serving neighbors.

Saying we believe we work for the good of our neighbors is not going *Last to Least*. Remember the story I told way at the beginning about my first and only rotation after PA school? That story reminded me of way that off-handed comment by the attending physician changed my vocational perspective. To hear that doctor admit it was wrong to prescribe antibiotics to a person with a virus, then say "If they don't get it here, they will go somewhere else," was hardening. If we say we believe that our work is for the good of others, but then we always benefit from transactions at their individual or collective expense, we are fooling ourselves. Even if we decide *Last to Least* is the best way to manage ourselves, we may find it will be an acquired taste. What can we do to acquire the appetite for *Last to Least*? What road signs keep us moving toward the target of the needs of our neighbor? What rules can we live by that create a strong identity and keep us moving toward neighbors-guided work even when we rationalize money or approval is best at the moment?

QUESTION #3: HOW DO I DO IT?

Now that we know the answer to Question #2, "Who achieves neighbors-guided work?" we can move to question #3. Remember, the order is as important as the questions. If we go directly to the rules before we develop the character traits, we may find ourselves unable to stick to the rules. If we learned the rules without answering the first question, "What is the guiding purpose of work?" we could find ourselves employing the rules to get approval or make more money. In that case, we might say, "If you take care of needs, the money will come flying in." That statement may actually be true, but that is not the way I am proposing we manage ourselves. I would definitely rather do business or pay for services from someone who has my best interest in mind, but we will steer ourselves into frustration if we do not remember the difference in means and ends.

The order matters.

However, here we are! We have arrived finally at the question we want answered, and having answered #1 and #2, we are ready to ask #3. To review:

1. What is the guiding purpose of work?

2. Who achieves that purpose?

3. How do they do it?

Ready to get started? Let's do it!

SERVE WITH A COST

There is no question that the good of my neighbor is the point of my sacrifice, but when I am wondering if I am truly going *Last to Least*, serving with a personal cost is a good way to refocus my attention. So, for our first road sign, we should ask, "When is the last time I served without calculating the gain for myself?"

The goal is always mutual benefit. However, we must acknowledge there will be times we must sacrifice the things that benefit ourselves to truly serve someone else. It may be the smallest gesture or a grand sacrifice, but there should be times when we do not consider our own interests if we are to strive after *Last to Least*.

Peter Drucker gave an interesting illustration of President Truman in *Management Challenges for the 21st Century*. He says Truman was picked for the vice-presidency because he was totally concerned with domestic issues. After becoming President, he went to the Potsdam conference and sat between Stalin and Churchill. After that experience, Truman realized foreign policy would have to dominate his presidency, but he knew little about it and was uninterested in learning. Truman had to put the good of the country above his own desires. Drucker claims it was Truman, not Stalin or Churchill, who created the postwar world with his leadership. He did not want to be a "foreign policy" president, but he realized the neighbors he had promised to serve needed him to lay aside his interests for theirs.[53]

I wonder if he came to love his new focus. I know it happened to me. I have experienced great joy by learning what the people in my field need and trying to fill that need. You can start doing this today, and it can change any vocation. If you cannot recall sacrificing for someone in a while, let this be your sign, like Joe's speed limit. Do something for someone and do not let another person in the world know about it. If you are a manager, give someone you manage time off and take up a project for them. If you are a solicitor, believe someone you may normally pre-judge. If you are a salesman, give someone advice about a product they do not buy from you. These are not everyday occurrences, but if you find yourself unwilling to do these simple tasks, it is an indication that you are like Joe going 75 in a 50 and justifying it because he is trying to help someone move a load. This road sign keeps us putting the needs of neighbors at the center of our work even when we are tired or frustrated. The sign "serve with a cost" keeps us going *Last to Least*.

CELEBRATING INSTEAD OF
TOLERATING AUTHORITY

Early in my career, I worked for an accomplished leader who had confidence in his abilities. I was also volunteering in another organization. I had always known I was opinionated, but I would have never considered myself to have a problem with authority. I was terribly wrong.

I had also begun to spend time with an older gentleman who I first thought of as an accountability partner, but he later started to give me homework assignments, and it developed into a mentorship. I was thinking about authority and wrestling with my relationship with it when I realized something embarrassing. The only three people in the world who I felt uncomfortable around were the three people with authority in my life. When I say uncomfortable, I mean when I entered a room with them, there was tension inside me. I became aware of everything I was saying and wondered what they thought about my words and actions. I did not think they appreciated the contribution I was making to the organizations they were leading. I thought they were often being selfish. I thought about all the things I would do differently if I were in their positions, and it gave me anxiety to think about being under their leadership for a long period.

I would often daydream about what it might be like if I went to another job or volunteered somewhere else. I was managing myself with me at the center of everything. When I realized this, it was another true confrontation moment. I knew I could justify myself by pointing out the flaws of the one of these leaders. Every leader has flaws, so we can easily find a reason to discount their leadership in our lives because of some shortcoming we see in them. Because *Last to Least* is a system of self-management, some may think authority would be rebelled against or at least avoided. However, our leaders are our neighbors as well! They are trying to accomplish objectives and put pieces together we may not always see. Their actions may seem selfish to us when they do not put our interests first.

The truth is, the problem is our own. In this case, the problem was mine. It is not unreasonable for a leader to put my needs second, or third, or fourth when he is solving an organizational problem. Surely, I can admit I am not privy to all the information informing his decision.

We should consider the needs of as many people as we can, but leaders realize some decisions will not be immediately optimal for every person involved. Take promotions, for example. I have been promoted in my organization, but I have also been passed over for a promotion. At the time, I felt like I was the most qualified candidate, or I would not have applied. When I didn't get the position, I could manage myself by turning inward or going *Last to Least*. I could question how the people in authority could ever make a decision like that and question their leadership skills. Or, I could trust the position of the leader and consider the hopes and dreams of all people involved.

This *neighbors-guided* approach can change everything. What if you began to think about how the promotion you didn't get affected the other people who had applied? What if you considered their families and the impact receiving a promotion may have on them?

"I can't help how I feel, can I?" I have been asked countless times. Maybe not directly, but indirectly I think we can. If we celebrate the protection that authority brings, we can enjoy the release of the responsibility. I do not have to consider every minor decision those with authority over me have made. I can rest in acceptance instead of following with dissent and dissatisfaction.

Isn't this opening the door for abuse? Sure, it could. I am never saying accept abuse. However, consider this. Is accepting authority equivalent to being abused? Absolutely NOT. Learning to celebrate authority does not necessarily lead to abuse. Simply because failing to challenge authority COULD lead to oppression does not mean it ALWAYS does. Learning to celebrate authority can protect us from leaving a great situation too soon. It can give us the direction we need when we are still learning or too emotionally attached to a situation to steer ourselves clearly without help. Take a moment to consider how much pressure would be removed from your shoulders if you decided to allow the leaders in your life the freedom to influence you.

You are still allowing the leadership, so you are managing yourself. You may already submit to authority because you think you have to in order to get ahead. Think about the difference it would make if you learned to celebrate authority instead of simply submitting.

DO NOT WITHHOLD TRUTH, BUT DO NOT WITHHOLD GOOD

While thinking through this concept, a friend in a similar position as myself called because he had not received a promotion. He was heading to a meeting and would soon face the leaders who made the decision to give the promotion to another candidate. "I know they are going to ask me if I am ok, and I just don't know what I am going to say. I am not ok," he lamented.

I had actually heard this concept at a marriage conference

with Scott and Dawn Smith. They counsel couples on building relationships and serving one another, but it applied perfectly to the situation. "You do not have to be inauthentic and you do not have to disrespect their authority, "I told him. "I would walk in with a big smile because even though you disagree, you are really ok. We both have better situations than we ever thought possible ten years ago."

"I agree with that," he said.

We can respect authority even when we disagree. We even be angry and still keep ourselves out of the center of the interaction.

"If they ask you," I said, "I would say, 'I disagree with the way this was handled, but I will not withhold good from you when it is in my power to do it.'"

My friend was feeling like he was the center of his work, and it was causing him great anxiety. Truly though, respect for authority does not mean we ignore when authority acts unjustly. If you need to confront someone for truly taking human rights, then going *Last to Least* means thinking of how many people will continue to be oppressed if you stay silent. However, if the authority in our lives is merely disagreeing with us, then going *Last to Least* means being followers who say why we disagree but continue to serve our leaders and clients with the same fervor we had when we realized our work was no longer about us.

Look what good can come of learning this self-management tactic when you become the leader. You will have ready examples when a team member gets angry or smug toward you. You will be able to empathize with them and lead them through the process.

I was managing a customer service rep who wanted to become an agent. This would be a promotion in our company, but I knew she was not ready. I was under some pressure because an agent I had just tried to hire had backed out days before his start date and we were short-handed. If we do not learn to manage ourselves with respect to authority, we will be hard pressed to lead someone else through the process. I was a little taken back when she started giving me the cold shoulder after I expressed my hesitation with her promotion. I had the same worst to first thoughts everyone has. I was tempted to feel like she needed to respect me, the boss, and just be thankful for a job. I did not want my impulses to manage me though, I want to manage myself. I gave myself the same advice I had given my friend who did not get the promotion.

I went to her and asked if anything was going wrong. I knew I would have to remain calm and be ready to absorb her anger. She finally began to cry and told me how she felt wronged. I was able to share some of my own disappointments, and then I gave her the truth and promised to not withhold good. "You are not ready," I told her, "but I am committed to helping you get ready. Let's meet every Tuesday in my office and go over situations this week where you were unprepared, and let's get you prepared."

I did not withhold the truth, but I did not withhold good from her. She came to the meeting weekly and as we practiced some of the tough conversations we have in serving people by helping them see needs, she flourished. During each step of the process, she learned to trust me because she was becoming more comfortable, confident and capable of a neighbors-guided way of managing herself. She was going from *Last to Least*.

Sometimes we will face a stressful situation and our character traits may not come out. We may need this road sign, "Do not withhold good OR truth" to keep us from wrecking our own career or the career of another. Usually we lean to one or the other until the character traits of *Last to Least* are fully developed (which takes a lifetime), so we need this reminder when we are tempted to go back to worst to first.

PURSUE RELATIONSHIPS ACROSS BARRIERS

I literally ugly cried when I read *Same Kind of Different as Me*.[54] The story is about Denver Moore and Ron Hall. Denver was a homeless African American man who forged a friendship with a rich, white art dealer. One of the most touching parts of the story for my wife was Denver telling about Mr. Ballentine, an 80-something white man in a nursing who Denver frequently visited even though Mr. Ballentine called him a derogatory word. She was touched by the unlikely relationship and an act of true service.

I think the spot where I ugly cried was surprising even to me, but it struck a chord with me deeply. The story began with Ron and Denver telling their own stories long before they ever met. Each chapter, or every couple chapters, would switch narrators. When I realized each of them, though coming from different places, were both winding up in Fort Worth Texas, I lost it! Hearing the story leading up to their meeting made me realize just how unlikely that meeting was. They met by only the slimmest of chances, and if the probable thing had happened, they would have never met one another. Unexpected events really get to me. Especially as it becomes clear there is a wise hand guiding the entire process. The fact these two strangers found one another was the most unlikely meeting but forged the most unbreakable friendship. There were so many barriers to their relationship, but somehow it survived and produced fruits that were unimaginable.

I think people are caught off guard when you reach across barriers. We have some glaring ones across the earth. Race keeps people divided as well as class. Sometimes sex is used to build walls between males and females. Language is a barrier no matter where you go. There are differences among any of the neighbors we choose to serve, but some of those differences are enjoyed and some are used to build walls. Reaching across barriers is another example of making ourselves uncomfortable that has the power to actually change our interests.

Here's an example that might be a little more accessible. I ate pineapple from a can my entire childhood. When we were married, my wife brought home fresh pineapple from the grocery store. I declined because, "I do not like pineapple." My perspective was skewed because of my previous experience. Pineapple is my favorite fruit today. If I had remained confident in my previous expectations of pineapple, I would have been unable to enjoy the amazing fruit the way it is intended to be enjoyed.

We all come from somewhere—profound, I know. But truly, we are entering into new relationships and encountering new possibilities every day with our previous experiences coloring every perception we have. We NEVER merely see things as they are because we come in with preconceived ideas that interact with our new experiences.

Take this as a road sign. If we developed the characteristics of someone who achieves neighbors-guided work, we would never need this sign, but we know our own past experiences, so sometimes we need to be reminded to reach across barriers.

Do not expect characteristics of the people you meet today to be like the people you learned to hate in the past. Do not expect the young man who walked in with a hat on to be a slacker because you know a slacker who wears a hat. Try to understand him and try to understand why the hat bothers you. If you are a leader in his life and the hat needs to go, tell him with the same gentleness with which you would like to be corrected. If the hat is your preference only, see if your neighbors may be served better because he wears it before making a demand.

If you have come to expect behaviors from a certain racial or socioeconomic group because "the stats don't lie," give the person dressed differently than you the opportunity to teach you something about themselves and yourself. You may be rejecting the "canned pineapple" when the real person in front of you is freshly positioned to help you and your organization flourish.

It is self-evident to most people today that a human has value because they are human. The neighbor you encounter today may have a hand only you can hold or a tear only you can dry. Please do not withhold your education or your advice or your service because that neighbor is different than you.

A practical way to go *Last to Least* is to think about the people or groups you or your organization would normally exclude and intentionally choose to serve them. When this concept was really starting to change my actions, I heard a story that inspired me.

A group of salesmen had to choose roommates on an incentive trip. A younger white qualifier named Joe decided to reach across a barrier to an older black winner, George. Joe knew how successful the George had been and wanted to get to know him. Joe emailed George and copied the person making the room assignments and asked if he would like to room with him. George actually never responded, but when they arrived, they were booked together. Joe knew there were some barriers between he and Joe, but he decided to reach across. He was worried that George may think it was weird that he asked to room with him since they did not know each other well, but he forget himself and reached.

Brene Brown, in *Braving the Wilderness,* talks about difficult conversations she has had with acquaintances. She says it is hard to hate from up close, so we should move in if we want to experience true belonging.[55]

The last morning, they started to leave, and Joe said something he was nervous to say, but he thought George would very much like to hear if someone meant it. Joe thought this because his close friend, who is an African-American man as well, told him he thought George would like to hear it. Joe and his friend had talked extensively about racial reconciliation, both being passionate about healing the wounds of our country and both being convinced it could only happen with small seemingly insignificant reaches across barriers. Joe called his friend and asked him to help him think through how he could reach across to George and then put it into practice.

"Has it been tough as a black man to be in such a white organization for so long?" Joe asked George.

George seemed relieved to be asked. He reported how he had really just accepted the fact that comments would be made, and he would just decide to take it and do a good job. George is a savvy businessman, owning many properties as well as being successful in sales for years. The conversation turned to religion, and they talked through a few big concepts regarding meaning and purpose.

George said, "All right Joe. You are a Christian. Do you believe all men are created equal?"

"I do," he replied.

"You have girls, right?" George raised his eyebrows a little.

"Sure do." Joe said.

George leaned forward like an attorney about to blow open the case. "Would you be ok if one of those girls married a black man?"

"Absolutely," Joe smiled.

He had almost formed, "Mm hmm," on his lips as if he had caught Joe in an existential contradiction. When he heard "absolutely," his eyes softened as he sat back on the couch.

"A lot of people say they are Christians, but they would never allow their girls to be with a black man, and the same is true for a lot of black fathers with their daughters marrying whites."

Joe was becoming different while they talked. There are tears running down my cheeks as I remember this simple beautiful story. Like Joe, I picked up on the notion to distrust black men growing up. Nobody sat me down and told me not to trust, but it was clear in my community there should be a healthy distance between white and black. Sure, we could play basketball together or visit one another's church, but even spending the night was something I never did. When a black coach married a white woman, I heard people worry out loud about the example it would set for the students. There is no basis for thinking that couples from different races should not marry, but that thought is common across the world. That is my canned pineapple, but this conversation between Joe and George is the real thing.

We are going to hit barriers. If I am in the center of my self-management, I will always try to make myself more comfortable or prouder and when I do, my neighbor loses out. I believe we all lose out. Even if I am nervous, or anxious, or have legitimate excuses to pull back from others, I can follow through by going straight at the barrier and putting the needs of my neighbor first.

A good friend confronted me about trying to purposefully get to know someone of a different race. "You are being racist as anyone when you do that," she said, "You should not seek someone out because of their race. That is racist."

Is it? The definition of racism includes the belief one race is superior to another. I do not believe one race is superior to another. Acknowledging there are barriers and fighting to tear down the barriers has a similarity with racism. In both scenarios you acknowledge that people have different races, but you act differently. It would be like saying that there is no difference between imprisoning the innocent and freeing the innocent because both involve the innocent.

As uncomfortable as it can be, I focus on race because it is such a consistent tension in our culture, but the barriers are many. You may not see how anyone could ever be so ignorant as to withhold working relationships from another race and you are right to feel that way. Beware, though, some of the most bigoted people I know are those who feel superior to bigots. They hate people who feel superior to others and deem them less than human. These types of people are doing exactly what they are so turned off by. Reach across barriers to any group you feel detached from and do it because you want to serve them and connect with them, not to simply exploit them for profits.

Intentionally putting ourselves in close spaces with people we have been sorted from previously is a practical way to go *Last to Least*. In managing ourselves, we can continue to think about how we will look or how we will be uncomfortable when we approach barriers with others. The benefits of getting to know others who are different, with different experiences are countless. I hope you see I have tried to stay away from focusing on benefits because benefitting oneself is not the focus of this book. In this case though, I think the benefits are a proper reward. Getting to know the experiences of others is like seeing the tops of clouds from an airplane for the first time. You knew they were majestic and beautiful, but you had never seen them from this angle! The human experience is one to be shared. Do not exclude neighbors from your work and your work will be everything it was meant to be!

SET ALARMS WHEN YOU PROMISE TO SHOW UP

I would laugh if this was the section most people benefit from in this entire book, but I would not be surprised if it is. Doing what we promise to do is essential when we are managing ourselves with others at the center. We must know the difference in two words: trustable and trustworthy.

Trustable describes a person who seems like they can be trusted.

Trustworthy describes a person that actually can be trusted.

When I meet a prospective client ,they have no idea if I am trustworthy. We have all heard people say, "I can just tell about people," but the truth is sometimes we cannot. On the other hand, how many of the people you know are trustworthy could convince someone else they actually are? Everyone I lead knows the difference between these two powerful words and knows how important they BOTH are.

If you are trustable, but not trustworthy, you will be using your gifts and skills to manipulate others for your good. You may have a flash of success followed by a trail of disappointment. Or worse, you may go your entire life and never be caught and become convinced all of life really is about you. How sad and miserable that would be.

If you are trustworthy, but not trustable, you will never convince your neighbor their needs can be trusted with you. You will be honest and ready to help, but probably never have the impact you could because you cannot communicate your ability to be trusted.

That was a long introduction to say we should set alarms when we promise to be somewhere. When I began to look for the needs of my neighbor at work, I also started to look for needs close to where I live. I met my friend Jerry at a Christmas parade. My neighborhood has parties and only invites the people who live past the gate. I am not saying there is a problem with that, but I told my wife I would like to get to know all the people who lived near us, not just those most like us in our neighborhood. So, I asked Jerry to lunch and we decided to plan a community potluck.

Jerry is an amazing storyteller. He puts his whole body into the story and usually takes off his jacket if he feels like the point is really sinking in. I would pick Jerry up for some of our meetings. He was really honest with me about a tough personal and work history. One of the things I noticed is when we would say we were going to leave at 7:30 am, I would call to let him know I was on the way (we live five minutes apart) and he would wake up with my phone call. I would often sit and wait five to ten minutes before we left. One day after we had eaten lunch together, we walked outside and planned to see each other at 7:30 on Sunday morning. I grabbed my phone and told Siri, "Remind to go get Jerry at 7:15 Sunday morning!" Jerry grabbed his phone and said, "Set an alarm for 7:30 on Sunday to go with Casey." As you can see, there was a little more coaching needed. I had to tell him that I already had another alarm that would wake me up to get ready. This new alarm would simply remind me to pick him up. He smiled and set a new alarm for 6:45.

Do you know I had never thought of setting myself reminders on my phone until I saw a friend of mine do it? Now I do it for every meeting. I set reminders to pick up the kids on days when I need to leave early because my wife needs me at home early. I set reminders to post my weekly and monthly reports. I set reminders to call back clients and to remember lunch appointments. I wish I could say I never miss anything. I still do, but this simple tactic has allowed me to be involved in many areas at one time.

Some days my phone annoys me to death. The amount of information that is required to manage oneself well is astounding. I could never remember everything I have promised to do. This simple act of setting reminders has made me more trustable, as well as more trustworthy. I do not want to lie to anyone, that is my true heart, but I also have serious memory limitations. Even if we feel like we can be trusted to the fullest extent, we become less trustable when we promise to do something and then fail to deliver. The reason we do not deliver what was promised may be acceptable, but we become less trustable, nonetheless. When we realize our memory limitations, still make the promises, but do not show up, we are actually becoming less trustworthy. A simple reminder keeps us admitting our limitations and showing up when we promised!

ACCEPT SURPRISES AS OPPORTUNITIES

In our current work where we are all moving people and increasingly becoming knowledge workers, we have to learn to manage ourselves when surprised. I created a call sheet many of the agents in my company have now reported they use regularly. That sheet is very simple but has proven extremely helpful. When I am tired, busy, or in a hurry, I can always move back into worst to first, but this call sheet reminds me to manage myself when surprised.

One of our main goals in serving our neighbors is making face-to-face meetings. We believe people are more likely to see their own situation when we meet face-to-face. It helps us communicate non-verbally and ask more questions when people appear uneasy or confused. Looking someone in the eye allows me to help people see things that would have otherwise gone unnoticed.

Last to Least is measuring where I have influence and accepting where I am powerless. *Last to Least* is knowing the difference between watering and growing fruit. We fully accept we are powerless to sell anything without a neighbor who is willing to buy. That is why I created the call sheet to measure where we have influence. I will first remind you how I use it to get all the way to what I can control and then show you how it is used to accept surprises as opportunities.

I will ask a room full of people, "Can you promise me you will sell just one application this week?" They think I am asking a small task, so they nod yes. "But you cannot," I tell them, "because you are powerless to make someone pay for that product." They are always a little stunned because no one in the sales management world wants to admit to their sales force they are powerless to do the very thing they are hired to do!

I go on, "So we cannot promise a sale, but we know how sales are generated most often, that is face-to-face interviews. We know usually four interviews turns into one sale on average, so can you promise me four interviews this week?" I ask with a big smile.

Almost always people look like they have seen the light and shake their head affirmatively and are quickly disappointed. You cannot promise four people will choose to come into your office this week. When managing ourselves, there is always internal tension when we put pressure on ourselves to do what we know we cannot be sure we can do. So finally, on average we ask 32 people before four say yes to an interview. "Can you promise that you will ask 32 people to come in for a face-to-face interview?" Absolutely you can.

That was all recap. We are already convinced that in self-management we measure watering, not growth only.

The new question is, where do the 32 people come from? Agents tell me how busy they are receiving phone calls from members who need to change vehicles or had a child move out or start driving or bought a new house. There is so much going on, we cannot get to making the calls for these face-to-face interviews.

"What if I told you I almost always set interviews with people who call me?" I ask. The surprises on the phone are opportunities to use your work to serve! I will tell our agents these interruptions are the very people who they are there to serve. They do not have to stay late three nights each week to offer 32 interviews, but they can offer them to the people who call for other services.

A person calling unexpectedly can distract me from a productive process, or I can accept the surprise as an opportunity to offer the other products I am working hard to sell. This reverse marketing technique is essential to those of us who simultaneously service and sell. And truly, we all are. Teachers are constantly being interrupted by student questions while they are preparing or lecturing. Would you see that surprise from a student as an opportunity to enlighten or as unwanted distraction? Health care administrators are surprised by changes in initiatives from the board of directors. Would you see this as frustration? You could accept the surprise as an opportunity to persuade them based on current progress or you could see an opportunity to start in a fresh direction.

Still, many agents say, "Ok, Casey. I am going to really start making these extra calls and stay late if I need to. I am going to get to 32."

These agents cannot see the surprises are opportunities. About the third time I say it though, it's like a light bulb goes off. One agent said, "I am going to redouble my efforts." I said, "If you think I am saying that, you are mishearing me. You need to refocus, not redouble your efforts."

Maintaining a clear focus on neighbors-centered work is best way to turn surprises into opportunities. When you work to avoid surprises, you become exhausted as you attempt to keep your hands around every situation, firmly in control. When you are trying to control every situation, you are not letting the needs of your neighbors steer your actions, but the needs of yourself.

Last year I had a good friend who needed some help with his immigration status. I knew my friend Jojo had a connection with a person who ran a ministry that specifically existed to help people through the difficult task of citizenship. Jojo is the leader of a local religious organization. He is involved with community outreach as well as fundraising for the services they provide.

I called Jojo and after a friendly exchange, I told him what the call was about. He offered to help my friend if I would just text him his contact info. I thanked Jojo and just before we got off the phone, he said, "Hey, before you go, what do you have going on next Thursday?" I was not sure but asked him why. "I need a few more teams for our annual golf fundraiser and I know you play. Would you be interested in getting a team together or sponsoring a hole?"

That situation could have gone very differently. Imagine Jojo at his desk calling on donors and raising money to serve the neighbors in his organization. Then, he gets a surprise call from me. If Jojo is managing himself according to worst to first, he would immediately be angry that I interrupted his productive time to ask him to do a favor for my friend. He rushes through the call and is now bitter that his time has been wasted. Imagine the next three calls are to donors who cannot or will not give this year. Jojo's frustration climbs, and he decides to quit for the day because everyone is only interested in themselves, not what he needs to do. Can't you see that happening in your own world?

But, what did he do instead? He saw the surprise as a unique opportunity to continue to serve all the neighbors in his field of influence. He served my friend, he served his organization, and he served me by opening my eyes to an opportunity I was unaware of minutes earlier.

When I was writing this section of the book, I took a trip to Lake Tahoe. The stunning snow-capped mountains and blue water were as breathtaking as the altitude. I rode with two others on the trip, so we stood in the TSA line together at the airport. At one point, they went left and I was directed to go right by a TSA agent. We agreed to meet at the gate. I had been redirected into a line trying to complete a Guinness Book World Record for the slowest TSA line ever. The man in front of me moved like he was underwater, the lady checking the bags really took her time. I think it was her first day on the job because she kept asking the other computer operator to look at her screen. My temperature rose and when my bag was held for inspection, I completely lost sight of the neighbors around me.

I started thinking about how silly I would look to my co-workers, then snatched my bag from the agent's hand and bolted. The other agents were texting me, asking where I was because they had been at the gate for such long time. I arrived with the door still open, but the attendant would not let me in the door.

"Only I could manage to ride with others and be the only person to miss the flight." I thought, and I was angry. The negative self-talk came flooding in. "They think you are irresponsible. They are probably saying, 'Yes, we expected that out of Ryals.'"

Maybe they were saying those things, and maybe they were right. I could have arrived earlier. Then I thought about my neighbors. I thought about the people who will read this book. Few or many, I thought about those who will read how *Last to Least* had literally breathed life into the dead bones of my vocation. I took out my computer and realized I would now have the entire day in the airport to serve you well. In my research that day, I discovered how to best communicate what *Last to Least* actually is: a self-management system. Before that day, I knew all the concepts of *Last to Least*, except I knew it needed a better descriptor. I had told so many people it was not a leadership book, but it was more about "how to work personally." It was in the airport on that day I found Peter Drucker's article, "Managing Oneself" which helped me clarify this is a system of self-management. That is a surprise I will be forever thankful for, but I almost missed it because I was tempted to be consumed with my own frustration instead of seeing an opportunity to prepare to serve anyone who will read this book!

MANAGE YOURSELF RATHER THAN
BEING MANAGED BY YOURSELF

A quick read of the Oxford Encyclopedia will show self-talk is widely studied. The overview shows many scientific studies have been done and some of the results are in direct contradiction of one another. I am obviously not saying I have the authority to weigh in on the massive debate around positive and negative self-talk and the effects it has on performance. I can, however, say those who go *Last to Least* talk to themselves instead of listening to themselves. When I took an employee with me to make a sales call, I wanted her to listen first and then try to take the lead at the second stop. We got in the truck on the way back to the office and talked about what just happened. I have had similar talks with my brother after he prices a load of rock for a new client or makes a deal with a vendor for services we need. These post-work meetings are essential when we are trying to develop the skill of managing ourselves or teaching others to do the same. There are versions of this in every industry.

"How did you feel when you were talking with him?" I asked her.

"I felt like he was thinking I was dumb the entire time," she said, "I mean I was ok with it, but I think he was just kind of intimidating." She tried to make sure she did not look too weak.

That negative thought is what steered her through the conversation. Do you see the danger here? If he sees we can help him in an area where she is less knowledgeable then she has to decide, "Do I help him, or do I look smart?" In that moment she was not tethering to his needs, but she was listening to herself instead of managing herself. When those going *Last to Least* have these worries about looking incapable or being intimidated, they do not shy away from the neighbor's need! No, they tell themselves, "I want to look knowledgeable, but looking knowledgeable is not why I showed up here today. Serving needs is!"

When you have a meeting and all the big players in your industry or organization are represented, will you be managed by the voice that says, "You need them to see you," or rather, "They will not notice you." No, do not listen to yourself on that! You will either walk into the room with a false confidence that makes others uncomfortable, or you will shrink into the corner and regret your paralysis. We are all uncomfortable in these spaces. If we never go into new and uncomfortable spaces, we have become the big fish in a small pond.

What if we went in, not to be made comfortable, but to acknowledge the need for others to be comfortable! Now I am approaching others, so they do not need to put on their false confidence. Now I am approaching those on the edges dying to talk to someone because they need to be comforted! Those going *Last to Least* will have the courage to approach those on the fringes with the humility to bring others into the conversation. You need to talk to yourself about the needs of others. I want to be in a room where people are managing themselves this way. I want to be approached with a pitch by someone talking to themselves this way. We obviously talk to ourselves positively and negatively. I want to change the aim of the positive and negative self-talk.

My very first client who I took through the 6-week course associated with *Last to Least* had similar thoughts when speaking to potential investors in his start-up or other strategic partners. He actually took his idea to audition for *Shark Tank*. At this point he has received one call back, so I am not sure if he will make it or not. We talked through this section the week after he returned from the first audition. He said, "I wish we had gone through this last week!"

He told me how he was constantly worried about what the judges thought of him and that he felt like it weakened his pitch. We both agreed early that he was tethered to approval with his work. He was looking for an identity as a successful entrepreneur. When we were talking about the power of *Last to Least* in situations where we are being "sized up," he realized the power *Last to Least* has to change his life. Throw out, "How do I look?" and ask yourself, "How can I help?" Throw away, "I can do this!" for "I can serve them!" Toss, "You may never get this opportunity again!" for "They may not get another chance to hear this!" Trade, "Just a few more hours and I can rest," for "Just a few more hours and their needs are met!"

ACCEPT THE LIMITATIONS OF OTHERS

Work can be discouraging! If every person bought our products, every patient followed our advice, every employer appreciated our contribution, and every employee appreciated our leadership, there would be little need for self-management. We are all part of a system and contribute regularly to a system of work that is flawed. We all agree "no one is perfect."

Why then, do we sometimes manage ourselves as if we believe they should be?

We all agree we are not flawless, but the gremlins of shame get the best of us when we tell ourselves we should have been. Those who are developing into the kind of person who goes *Last to Least* have to admit we consistently fail to achieve this amazing aim! When others fail around me or when I fail myself, discouragement is the voice that says, "This will never work." I will never get buy in from investors. I will never change the culture of this company. We agree no one is perfect, but when we or someone around us actually makes a mistake, we think our collective limitations are going to keep us from achieving!

I am convinced that learning to accept the limitations of those around them is the secret to the success of some of our brightest business leaders! In a 2014 shareholder meeting, Warren Buffett was asked about his weaknesses. Buffett said as a manager, he can be "sloppy." "A pure weak point is, I'm slow to make personnel changes," he said. "There will be times when what you might call our lack of supervision of our subsidiaries means we'll miss something."[56]

Notice the context and remember he has the power to change how he makes personnel changes. If Buffett decided to change his strategy tomorrow, he has the power to do so. Why then does he admit this weakness, but fail to do something differently? Why does he allow personnel to remain the same even though they have obvious limitations? Because the successor of his personnel would have limitations as well. The next person you hire will have limitations! The person who hired you has flaws.

How would our businesses change if we were guided by the road sign that the limitations of others are a normal part of doing business? If we were fully changed by *Last to Least*, we would never lack the humility needed to accept others' limitations. The reason we fail to accept the limits of others is we fail to remember our own!

Buffet knows something many know, but do not have the courage to admit. Or at least we do not have the courage to act as if it is true. We do not know the exact "right" time to break a relationship in the context of work. We cannot always be sure this manager will never change or that co-worker is stuck in her ways, or that employee refuses to learn. We feel tension when in these scenarios because we vacillate between, "They will never change," and "This may turn out for the good!" Buffet knows we either have to choose to over-trust or under-trust.

"Well, why don't we just trust the perfect amount and terminate relationships at the "right" time?" you ask. Really? If someone could figure that out, don't you think Buffett would be the very one who could?

We lose customers because, "We do not have to deal with their unreasonable ways!"

We lose employees because, "They will never fit into this system!"

We leave employment because, "That manager does not understand!"

We find ourselves on the island of our own self-approval and far enough away to protect ourselves from these annoying people who cannot frustrate us any longer. We also find ourselves, to continue the allegory, far enough away from the mainland that we have no contact with those our work was actually designed to serve. We have no customers to serve so we close the doors. We have no employees because we found out that everyone has their limits, which we learned in the confrontation. We have no career because we bounce from place to place never truly becoming proficient.

Until we learn we need others to make allowances for our own imperfections, we will find it impossible to endure the deficiencies of others. So how do I set up a road sign to manage being discouraged by the limitations of myself and others when going *Last to Least*? Two things become extremely important. First, I need reminders that everyone has limitations. Second, I need to look for times to expose, not disguise, my self-centeredness.

Having other people who see how a community, city, nation, or world would thrive if we centered our work around the needs of our neighbors is essential when we are discouraged. We need someone to remind us of the target when we start to become frustrated. I remember when I started taking this transformation seriously. I realized that although I was trying, I was still becoming frustrated and disillusioned.

I thought, "I am trying to really put my neighbor first, but I am not becoming the leader I want to be! I am not becoming as selfless as I thought I would be by this point!" Isn't it funny how it is so easy to slip right back into that type of thinking? I needed to be reminded that my leadership skills were not the focus. The needs of the people I am trying to lead are the center. I need a reminder that the aim is not my development, but my development is a means to an end of being prepared to fully meet the needs of my neighbors!

I know a young mother who has made a similar comment about her work. "I am not developing as a parent!" she said after a period of focus on parenting skills. So, I asked her if the point of her studies were to "develop as a great parent" or to "develop your girls into great adults." The means of learning the skills serve the ends of raising better children. If I cannot keep that clear in my mind, there will always be undue tension.

When we are discouraged, it may be because we are jumping back to hitting the target of self! When the young parent and I began to look at the true aim of her parenting, her girls, we discovered she was absolutely seeing results in her children! She thought she was failing because she had turned inward, but she was actually succeeding at the main purpose. As any parent knows, children do not learn immediately. We have to accept their limitations. When the young lady began to accept she would still have to correct behaviors tomorrow even though she had already disciplined her children today, she was relieved of the frustration of expecting more than they were capable of.

I interviewed an educator who had been teaching for over 25 years. I was talking with her about this concept. "Would teachers around you be less frustrated and disappointed if they learned to accept the limitations of those around them?" I asked.

"Of course!" she exclaimed. "I have to take into account that students come into my class at all different levels. I do not expect them to jump on grade level or jump ahead in creativity when I give them one instruction. I have to continue to teach day after day and never give up on them when they do not get it!" I love that she illustrated this concept perfectly and then added, "I can NEVER give up on them."

Accepting limitations is not about leaving people where they are. Do you see? This is why we also need people around us to encourage us to keep changing. The people around you need that encouragement. We cannot buy the lie that we are either challenging people to be great OR accepting their limits. No! We have to challenge one another AND accept that the relationship will last even if you have flaws.

We need like-minded people around us to remind us what we try not to see about ourselves. This is tough when you do not like feedback or are overly sensitive to criticism. However, it is essential to recognize that criticism and feedback are necessary to develop as a person. You will never begin to see this road sign to accept the limitations of others until you are able to admit that even you need others to accept your failures.

The second way we can learn to accept the limits of others is to quickly admit, not hide, our own. When someone offers criticism, we should open our ears and thank them heartily! We should remember they have limitations as well! When someone offers criticism of the way we are working, they are not necessarily good ideas. If we are always quickly jumping to defend ourselves, though, we will miss the needed advice that could make us more useful to our neighbors. On the other hand,—and this hurts us—they may be perfectly correct! Our critics may be pointing out a real flaw we can begin to work on. These criticisms may come from a friend or a leader. The advice may come from an employee. It may even come from an enemy. But being ready to quickly admit our own limitations will train us to be able to accept others like Buffet has trained himself to do.

We will find ourselves, like Buffett, enjoying the shared successes of those around us who we did not cut out of our circle too soon! There comes a time when the good of our neighbors is at stake if we partner with certain people. There is a time to terminate employment for the good of the entire community. However, I want my "weakness" to be that I bear with others too long, rather than that I cannot trust others to serve along with me!

FIND A NEUTRAL FACE

"I have a confession," a gentleman involved in an organization I was working with said to me a little sheepishly. "When I asked you about your thoughts on homosexual men, I told you I had a gay uncle. It was actually my dad."

I could feel him watching my face for any indication of what I was thinking. All I was actually thinking was what my friend Nicole taught me. Nicole has her Master's in professional counseling. She and my friend Aaron run a non-profit counseling center near St. Simons Island. I had always thought that I should smile at my clients when I was actively listening. I would nod my head to make sure they knew I was paying attention. Then Aaron and Nicole set me straight.

In their time as addiction counselors in Cleveland, they realized that a neutral face was vitally important when hearing controversial or private information. The reason this is important is because you have no idea what the person sharing the information associates with a simple head nod or a smile. We all know how important non-verbal communication is, but I had never heard much about my neutral face, so I wanted to include it in this section. They found in counseling, that the best way to receive private information was with a neutral face.

They taught me that when they did speak, they could clearly communicate with words, what they ACTUALLY thought about the information that was shared with them. There was less room for interpretation and therefore, more opportunity for clarity.

When my acquaintance told me this information there were hundreds of variables. We live in an era of "agree and love" or "disagree and hate," so I am sure he was wary of my reaction. I wanted his interpretation of my reaction to be my actual reaction. I also know we are all viewing one another through the lenses of our past experiences.

I was sure he trusted me with the information because the first conversation about his "uncle" had already taken place. At the same time, he obviously felt the need to keep this information from me before, so it was a guarded part of his story. I was so thankful to be equipped with my neutral face so I could hear him out and then respond with greater clarity.

Minding your nonverbal communication is an essential piece of managing yourself well. When a client or teammate reveals information about their families, history, or finances, they are watching your response closely. I have to ask invasive questions about my client's finances. Sometimes, I confess I have been shocked by what I have found. Sometimes, clients have expected me to be shocked when I am not at all. It is in these moments where trust can be built or shattered.

My acquaintance knows some people who would be repelled by knowing his father is in a homosexual relationship. He knows others who would view him differently because of this news. He was watching intently to see if he could see any of those reactions in my face as he told me. Our clients, students, and patients are watching us in the same way.

Would you rather them have to interpret your facial expressions, or would you rather them feel heard completely and then hear your words describe your response? Imagine my acquaintance sharing his news and I respond with a head nod up and down while pinching my eyebrows together and flattening my lips. I would mean, "Yes, I hear you and I am so thankful that you trust me enough to tell me the truth. I want you to know I am listening and that our relationship means the world to me." However, he may see me through the lens of a previous person he told the same information. He may take the same facial expression to mean, "I am so sorry you are having to deal with this tragedy." He may now feel like I view him differently because, in his estimation, I view this as a tragedy. He would have missed what I meant entirely, and words would have had to overcome this communication deficit.

While facial expressions work incredibly like salt to season the words, they are confusing as the main course. The expression of my face uncoupled with words to clarify what I mean is leaving my expression in the hands of my acquaintance's former experiences instead of the clear message I want to communicate.

For clarity's sake, a neutral face when hearing possibly controversial or uncomfortable information is important. Often, our responses in these situations are not simple. There are complex reactions that need to be explained. A simple smile or frown or nod up or look to the left cannot express the nuances that tough situations call for. A neutral face while listening will allow you to begin your response with a clean slate instead of depending on the perception of the person you are reacting to. Then, you will be able to communicate with your words AND your facial expressions, the clearest version of your response possible.

CELEBRATE OFTEN

One of the most difficult tasks as a sales manager trying to teach people to manage themselves according to *Last to Least* is commissions. It is an easy formula for an incentive to become the end itself rather than the means to the true end of serving. In a thoughtful organization, the highest commissions would be paid when the needs of the neighbors and communities we serve were met most comprehensively. Even when we realize this is true, it is difficult for some to unhear the "cha-ching" of the cash register whenever their client says "yes" to their good or service.

Many jobs also have bonuses attached when performance is high. Even those who are salaried or hourly employees have learned to celebrate the company making more and more money no matter if the customers win or lose. I have realized something though. No matter how conditioned we are to hear the cash register, no matter how many times someone says, "Money greases the wheel," no matter how much we have been conditioned to believe money is the purpose of work, we are still human, thankfully. We cannot deny the inextricable connection we have with one another. Therefore, I have noticed that there is also guilt associated with our celebrations.

We do not want to feel like the person running through the building saying "Got em!" when we make a sell. We do not like the feeling that we used someone for our own good. I have met those who will not excel at their work and if they rarely do, they do not want to celebrate the achievement. They rarely report these tweezed details without my constant questions, but there is guilt associated with achievement and they are not sure why.

The body shop down the street sure profited when we had a massive hailstorm last year. I know some real estate agents and investors who had massive gains when the housing market dropped, forcing many out of their homes. We do not want to ask others to be sad when they sell something or timid when they make an excellent business decision, but we also do not want to feel like we are celebrating talking someone into something for our gain.

The first and most obvious way to celebrate well is to be transparent and actually work for the needs of the neighbor. But some people still need a little push to celebrate because they are still cautious. Some should be more cautious. When we tell ourselves we are working for others, and then we celebrate the commissions we earned at each sale, there is tension and there may be guilt if we are truly seeking the good of our neighbor.

I had a new salesperson who felt this way. He had seen others celebrate their sales with cocky attitudes and shooting fingers and he wanted no part of it. He had lost some of the joy in truly helping others, because he was so cautious to never be like the others he felt were misguided. He had begun to lean into *Last to Least*, but I could tell he still had some hesitation to get excited when he had done a great job. I remembered some of the best advice I had been given. You have heard it before, but I want you to hear it in the context of truly celebrating what we are trying to accomplish here.

When I was a teenager, I would help my dad install vinyl siding on houses. We would have to be creative at some places because of the materials that were there previously. Most of his jobs were repairs or remodels, not new construction. There was no manual, so sometimes I was not sure if I was doing the job correctly. If I struggled to do the best I could for a first try, I would sometimes wonder if I should tear down the section I was working and start again. "How does this look!?" I would shout down from the scaffold, almost always exasperated. Without ever coming around the corner to see he would shout back, "How would it look if it was your house?"

Sometimes I would keep on going and others, I would start all over. The Golden Rule has a way to make situations seem simple and unambiguous. That is why when I started in the insurance business with the company my parents were insured by, their previous agent gave me similar advice. When he handed their file over to me, he said, "If you treat every account like you do this one, you will be incredibly successful."

We can celebrate with confidence when we are doing neighbors-guided work. No matter if we are teaching in the last period, seeing the final patient of the day, driving the final nail, or closing the sale, we are celebrating the small completion of something we were created to do. Work is not a curse, it is human! We do not just need the benefits of work to get the most out of our lives, we need the participation in work itself. I can celebrate and enjoy finishing the task, collecting the check, diagnosing the disease, collecting the test, moving the load, connecting the businesses, and making the sale because it is just the same as the feeling I got when I drove the final nail just before we "got up the tools". I got to step back and say, "If this was my house, I would be pleased and therefore I think the true owner will be too!"

The joy of driving the nail was for a job completed. A job completed that gave my neighbor pleasure in the product. That closed sale is no different if it is made going *Last to Least*. It is just the final nail in the process of the good of a neighbor. You would never say "got em" when driving the final nail. You would never say, "got em", if you were truly working for the good of your neighbor. You would, however, celebrate a job well done. A neighbor well served. I hope I never again lose the connection between a finished job and the neighbor I serve!

Going *Last to Least* will not answer every question or make every decision clear. My personal mission is to "encourage wisdom." Wisdom was a tough subject for someone like me to learn. Why? There are multiple solutions in wisdom. In science, we often try to control all variables other than those being tested. In human experience, though, there are just too many variables. Wisdom is choosing the best course of action given the current knowledge available. Sometimes there is not enough information to make the perfect decision. Other times, we know a better way, but are too tired or frustrated to take it. I readily admit *Last to Least* is not going to lead every organization into financial utopia. What I believe it could do is transform individuals and therefore communities and cities into places where we all want to do business!

CONCLUSION

I have saved the results for the end because it is tricky.

I hope you see that money, recognition, approval ,and identity are all woven into our work. I hope you also see that a met need necessarily comes before any of these in terms of importance. That is not a moral statement, but a wise statement. Wisdom is aligning ourselves with what is actually true. I hope you see that needs before profit is simply a best practice.

Executive Presence Without Arrogance

When you allow this wise way to work transform you, one of the most important benefits is what I call "executive presence." The people you lead need consistency. When they see you giving up temporary money or power to meet the needs of the neighbors and neighborhoods you serve, they will see a consistent leader who is not tossed by every impulse. The steadfastness they see in your leadership will bring them security and they will want to go where you lead.

When vendors know you put their needs first, they will be excited to refer others to you. When I see executive presence in an individual, I immediately ask if they are comfortable in their current role. Why? Because I want to hire them! When you walk into your next interview for a job or a promotion seeking to make others comfortable rather than wondering what they think about you, you will be amazed at the way you are received.

You may think it is magic, but it's not—it's wisdom. Forgetting yourself is not merely nice, it is wise.

The trap for most of us who gain executive presence is arrogance. If people begin to follow us, and those who lead us begin to praise and promote us, and vendors wants to sell to us, and customers want to buy, we get full of ourselves. The normal way executive presence is coached only exacerbates the problem. Normally, you are told to think more highly of yourself. Be proud of yourself when you walk in the room. Hold your head high with confidence. When you get executive presence this way, arrogance is lurking around the corner. Arrogance actually repels others and destroys the very presence you worked hard to gain.

However, when you seek to meet the needs of others and forget yourself, executive presence will naturally follow, sans that pesky arrogance.

Money

I never thought I would be able to make the amount of money I have made this far in life. I like it, but I could do without it tomorrow. My wife and I have found more joy in giving it away than I thought was possible. Giving away money is not merely nice, it is wise.

I wish I could find the article I read because this would be more powerful. But, years ago I read an article where the researcher interviewed 1000 millionaires. 90% of them reported that they made their money going after something besides money. They were following a guide besides money and the money trailed in behind them.

I really enjoy money, but you cannot enjoy it if you have to have it. If you can give it away or take it or leave it, then it will not act as a chain keeping you in one spot. You will make wise decisions because sometimes the next wise move will initially cost you. However, so many living Last to Least have found that when they seek to meet needs with their work and even meet needs with their money, they always have enough.

We all know the stats that find it is 5–7 times more expensive to obtain a new customer than to retain an existing customer.

When we meet needs before profits AND learn to communicate our mission to the community, they want to do business with us again and again. The money is not the guide, but the profits are made when you go Last to Least.

When we learn to meet needs with our work, we will be the most productive people in our organizations. The individuals I have led through this process have experienced over 100% increases in productivity year-over-year in their respective fields. Production brings about profit.

Happiness

One of the reasons I wrote this book is because of the impact that literature and advice has had in my own life. I cannot calculate the gratitude I have for self-help teachers and influencers.

However, I am unimpressed and frankly sick of hearing some of them tell people to just, "Do what makes you happy."

Victor Frankl was a Jewish psychiatrist and neurologist who spent three years in a Nazi concentration camp. In the 1946 book, *Man's Search for Meaning*, Frankl made a shocking statement to us. He said, "It is the very pursuit of happiness that thwarts happiness."[57]

You know this is true when you think about it, but let it change your actions this time. Think about what else he said: "Happiness cannot be pursued; it must ensue. One must have a reason to be happy."

A reason to be happy? Happiness automatically follows when you are seeking something meaningful. However, the moment happiness becomes the guide, it slips away from you. By working with the needs of others first, Last to Least helps you infuse meaning into any work, and happiness ensues.

Infusion happens in medicine when you receive IV medication. The medication enters the blood stream and mixes with your own fluids so that it becomes almost impossible to separate. You can infuse meaning into your work by going Last to Least in such a way that finding purpose in your work is inseparable from the job. You will never again be just taking vitals, making a sale, teaching a class, loading a truck, or cutting hair. You will be meeting the needs of the neighbors and neighborhoods. Please take the time to think about the needs you meet. Selling insurance is taxing. Encouraging the next wise move is meaningful. Seeing patients is monotonous. Healing wounds is meaningful.

It will be worth it for you. It will give you a reason to move. It will give you a new direction.

When you find meaning infused into the work itself, you will not need a break to pursue something meaningful, the meaning will come automatically in what you are already doing.

Final Thoughts

Imagine my wife, Alli, and her friend hiking up Mt. Yonah. Imagine Shelly was the guide, but Alli turned around and faced down the mountain and walked backward. Imagine our 8 year old, Livie was trailing behind Alli. Livie tells Alli when to turn left or right based on when Shelly does. Alli even looks over her shoulder every now and then to see what Shelly is doing, but she depends on Livie and continues to climb backward.

Alli would be frustrated with the hike. She may become frustrated with Shelly for turning without proper notice. She may be frustrated with Livie for failing to give clear instruction. She may fall frequently and it may take her twice as long to climb the mountain. She may never make it to the top because it's just too hard.

But if she simply turned around and walked in a new direction, Alli would be filled with life. She would follow Shelly up the mountain with grace and poise, and Livie would trail right behind.

When we work with a lesser guide than the needs of our neighbors, we are walking up the path backward. We may look to money or recognition, but reality is, even those things trail behind a need. We are sometimes hitting the path, but often we miss it all together. We feel like we missed something or made a wrong turn somewhere. We feel like we need a new job, new industry, or new customers. A change may help, but not until you change yourself first.

We need a new guide for our work. We should turn around, take a new direction, and fix our eyes on the needs of our neighbors and neighborhoods.

We will make our next wise move and the rest will trail behind!

ENDNOTES

1   Merriam-Webster, s.v. "capitalism," accessed December 10, 2019, https://www.merriam-webster.com/dictionary/capitalism.

2   Friedman, Milton. *Capitalism and freedom*. University of Chicago Press, 2009.

3   Harter, Jim, "Dismal employee engagement is a sign of global mismanagement," Gallup Blog, 2018, www.gallup.com/workplace/231668/dismal-employee-engagement-sign-globalmismanagement.aspx.

4   Harter, Jim, "Employee engagement on the rise in the US," Gallup News, August 28, 2018, https://news.gallup.com/poll/241649/employee-engagement-rise.aspx.

5   Godin, Seth, "The World's Worst Boss," Seth's Blog, December 4, 2010, https://seths.blog/2010/12/the-worlds-worst-boss/ (accessed December 17, 2019).

6   Wallace, David Foster, "This is Water" Kenyon College Archive, speech, Gambier, Ohio, May 21, 2005, http://bulletin-archive.kenyon.edu/x4280.html (accessed December 17, 2019).

7   Luke 15:11-13

8   Dostoevsky, Fyodor, 1821-1851. *The Brothers Karamazov*. New York: Vintage Books, 1950.

9   Saiidi, Uptin. "Millennials are Prioritizing Experiences Over Stuff." *CNBC*, May 5, 2016, www.cnbc.com/2016/05/05millenials-are-prioritizing-experiences-over-stuff.html (accessed December 17, 2019).

10   Eurhythmics, "Sweet Dreams (Are Made of This)," track 6 on *Sweet Dreams Are Made of This*, RCA Records, 1983, Album.

11   Luke 15:25-32

12   Erikson, Erik Homburger. "Identity and the life cycle: Selected papers." (1959).

13   Lewis, Clive Staples. *Mere Christianity*. Zondervan, 2001.

14   Keller, Tim. "The Advent of Humility." *Christianity Today* (2008): 50-53.

15   Hilgendorff, Gail. "Why do we Work So Hard? *Huffington Post*. Nov. 8, 2013, https://www.huffpost.com/entry/success-and-motivation_b_4236208 (accessed December 17, 2019).

16   Achor, Shawn. "The Happy Secret to Better Work," TedxBloomington, May 2011.

17   Smith, Larry, "Why You Will Fail to Have a Great Career," TedxUW, November 2011.

18   Alexander, Michelle. T*he New Jim Crow: Mass Incarceration in the Age of Colorblindness*. New York: New Press, 2010.

19   DiPaola, Steven. 2016-2017 Theatrical Season Report, Actor's Equity Association. www.actorsequity.org/aboutequity/annualstudy/2016-17-annual-study.pdf (accessed April 14,2019).

20   Plantinga, Alvin. *Warranted Christian Belief*. Oxford University Press on Demand, 2000.

21   Day, Doris. "Que Sera Sera," *Doris Day: Que Sera, 1956*.

22   Acts 27:20-32

23   Proverbs 21:31

24   Kroll, Luisa & Dolan, Kerry A., "Billionaires: The Richest People in the World," *Forbes*, March 5, 2019, www.forbes.com/billionaires/#37a67b3251c7

25   Ruelle, Peter, "Advance in high-pressure physics," *The Harvard Gazette*, January 26, 2017, news.harvard.edu/gazette/story/2017/01/a-breakthrough-in-high-pressure-physics/

26   Luckerson, Victor, "These Are The 10 Most Popular Tweets of All Time," *Time*, March 21, 2016, time.com/4263227/most-popular-tweets/

27   Brown, Brene, "Listening to Shame," March 16, 2012, https://www.ted.com/talks/brene_brown_listening_to_shame?language=en (accessed December 17, 2019).

28   *8 Mile*, directed by Chris Hanson, Imagine Entertainment, 2003.

29 Glucksberg, Sam, and Robert W. Weisberg. "Verbal behavior and problem solving: Some effects of labeling in a functional fixedness problem." *Journal of Experimental Psychology* 71, no. 5 (1966): 659.

30 Pink, Daniel H. *To sell is human: The surprising truth about moving others*. Penguin, 2013.

31 Drucker, Peter F. "Knowledge-worker productivity: The biggest challenge." *California management review* 41, no. 2 (1999): 79-94.

32 Drucker, Peter F. "Managing oneself." *Harvard Business Review* 83, no. 1 (2005): 100-109.

33 Ferry, Luc, translated by Theo Cuffe, *A Brief History of Thought*, (New York: Harper Collins, 2011).

34 Chopra, Deepak. *The path to love: Renewing the power of spirit in your life*. New York: Harmony Books, 1997.

35 Warren, Rick. *The purpose driven life: What on earth am I here for?*, Zondervan, 2012.

36 Piper, John. "Hope as the motivation of love: 1 Peter 3: 9–12." *New Testament Studies* 26, no. 2 (1980): 212-230.

37 *Batman Begins*, directed by Christopher Nolan. Burbank, CA: Warner Brothers, 2005.

38 Bellah, Robert Neelly, Richard Madsen, William Sullivan, Ann Swidler, and Steven M. Tipton. *Habits of the heart: middle America observed*. London: Hutchinson, 1985.

39 Brown, Robert McAfee. "Reinhold Niebuhr: A study in humanity and humility." *The Journal of Religion* 54, no. 4 (1974): 325-331.

40 Schwartz, Barry. *Why we work*. Simon and Schuster, 2015.

41 March, James G. *Primer on decision making: How decisions happen*. Simon and Schuster, 1994.

42 *Frozen*, directed by Jennifer Lee and Chris Buck, 2013; Burbank, CA: Walt Disney Pictures, film.

43 Stevenson, Bryan. *Just mercy: A story of justice and redemption*. Spiegel & Grau, 2019.

44 Duckworth, Angela, Grit: *The power of passion and perseverance*. Vol. 234. New York, NY: Scribner, 2016.

45   White, Jack E., "Martin Luther King," *Time*, April 13, 1998, accessed December 17, 2019 at http://content.time.com/time/magazine/article/0,9171,988163-2,00.html

46   King Jr, Martin Luther. "Keep moving from this mountain." *Address at Spelman College* (1960).

47   Sherry, Suzanna. "Lee v Weisman: Paradox Redux." *The Supreme Court Review* 1992 (1992): 123-153.

48   Schulaka, Carly. "Dan Pink on Why It's OK to Be in Sales, the Importance of Clarity, and a New Way to Innovate." *Journal of Financial Planning* 26, no. 9 (2013): 14.

49   ChurchPop, "Atheist Penn Jillette Doesn't Respect Christians Who Don't Evangelize," ChurchPop.com, https://churchpop.com/2016/01/16/atheist-penn-jillette-christians-evangelize/ (accessed December 17, 2019).

50   Chris Janson, "Buy Me A Boat," *Buy Me a Boat*, compact disc, March 20, 2015.

51   End Slavery Now, "Christine Caine: The A21 Campaign," EndSlaveryNow.org, https://www.endslaverynow.org/blog/articles/christine-caine-the-a21-campaign (accessed December 17, 2019).

52   Bryan Stevenson, "We Need to Talk About Injustice," June 8, 2016, https://www.youtube.com/watch?v=c2tOp7OxyQ8 (accessed December 17, 2019).

53   Drucker, Peter. *Management challenges for the 21st century*. Routledge, 2012.

54   Hall, Ron, and Denver Moore. *Same Kind of Different As Me Movie Edition: A Modern-Day Slave, an International Art Dealer, and the Unlikely Woman Who Bound Them Together*. Thomas Nelson, 2017.

55   Brown, B. *Braving the Wilderness: The Quest for True Belonging and the Courage to Stand Alone*, New York, Random House, 2017.

56   Warren Buffet Archive, "Morning Session—2014 Meeting, May 3, 2014 https://buffett.cnbc.com/video/2014/05/03/morning-session---2014-berkshire-hathaway-annual-meeting.html (accessed December 17, 2019).

57   Frankl, Viktor E. (2006) *Man's search for meaning* /Boston : Beacon Press.

BIBLIOGRAPHY

8 Mile, directed by Chris Hanson, Imagine Entertainment, 2003.

Achor, Shawn. "The Happy Secret to Better Work," TedxBloomington, May 2011.

Alexander, Michelle. *The New Jim Crow : Mass Incarceration in the Age of Colorblindness*. New York: New Press, 2010.

Batman Begins, directed by Christopher Nolan. Burbank, CA: Warner Brothers, 2005.

Bellah, Robert Neelly, Richard Madsen, William Sullivan, Ann Swidler, and Steven M. Tipton. *Habits of the heart: middle America observed*. London: Hutchinson, 1985.

Brown, Brene. *Braving the Wilderness: The Quest for True Belonging and the Courage to Stand Alone*, New York, Random House, 2017.

Brown, Brene, "Listening to Shame," March 16, 2012, https://www. ted.com/talks/brene_brown_listening_to_shame?language=en (accessed December 17, 2019).

Brown, Robert McAfee. "Reinhold Niebuhr: A study in humanity and humility." *The Journal of Religion* 54, no. 4 (1974): 325-331.

Chopra, Deepak. *The path to love: Renewing the power of spirit in your life*. New York: Harmony Books, 1997.

ChurchPop, "Atheist Penn Jillette Doesn't Respect Christians Who Don't Evangelize," ChurchPop.com, https://churchpop. com/2016/01/16/atheist-penn-jillette-christians-evangelize/ (accessed December 17, 2019).

Day, Doris. "Que Sera Sera," *Doris Day: Que Sera, 1956.*

DiPaola, Steven. 2016-2017 Theatrical Season Report, Actor's Equity Association. www.actorsequity.org/aboutequity/annualstudy/2016-17-annual-study.pdf (accessed April 14, 2019).

Dostoevsky, Fyodor, 1821-1851. *The Brothers Karamazov*. New York: Vintage Books, 1950.

Drucker, Peter F. "Knowledge-worker productivity: The biggest challenge." *California management review* 41, no. 2 (1999): 79-94

Drucker, Peter F. "Managing oneself." *Harvard Business Review* 83, no. 1 (2005): 100-109.

Drucker, Peter F. *Management challenges for the 21st century*. Routledge, 2012.

Duckworth, Angela, *Grit: The power of passion and perseverance*. Vol. 234. New York, NY: Scribner, 2016.

End Slavery Now, "Christine Caine: The A21 Campaign," EndSlaveryNow.org, https://www.endslaverynow.org/blog/articles/christine-caine-the-a21-campaign (accessed December 17, 2019).

Erikson, Erik Homburger. "Identity and the life cycle: Selected papers." (1959).

Eurhythmics, "Sweet Dreams (Are Made of This)," *Sweet Dreams Are Made of This,* RCA Records, 1983, Album.

Ferry, Luc, translated by Theo Cuffe, *A Brief History of Thought*, New York: Harper Collins, 2011.

Frankl, Viktor E. (2006) *Man's search for meaning* /Boston : Beacon Press.

Friedman, Milton. *Capitalism and freedom*. University of Chicago Press, 2009.

Frozen, directed by Jennifer Lee and Chris Buck, 2013; Burbank, CA: Walt Disney Pictures, film.

Glucksberg, Sam, and Robert W. Weisberg. "Verbal behavior and
    problem solving: Some effects of labeling in a functional fixedness
    problem." *Journal of Experimental Psychology* 71, no. 5 (1966): 65.

Godin, Seth, "The World's Worst Boss," Seth's Blog, December 4, 2010,
    https://seths.blog/2010/12/the-worlds-worst-boss/ (accessed
    December 17, 2019).

Hall, Ron, and Denver Moore. *Same Kind of Different As Me Movie
    Edition: A Modern-Day Slave, an International Art Dealer, and the
    Unlikely Woman Who Bound Them Together*. Thomas Nelson, 2017.

Harter, Jim, "Employee engagement on the rise in the US," Gallup News,
    August 28, 2018, https://news.gallup.com/poll/241649/employee-
    engagement-rise.aspx.

Harter, Jim, "Dismal employee engagement is a sign of global
    mismanagement," Gallup Blog, 2018, www.gallup.com/
    workplace/231668/dismal-employee-engagement-sign-
    globalmismanagement.aspx.

Hilgendorff, Gail. "Why do we Work So Hard? *Huffington Post*.
    Nov. 8, 2013, https://www.huffpost.com/entry/success-and-
    motivation_b_4236208 (accessed December 17, 2019).

Janson, Chris, "Buy Me A Boat," *Buy Me a Boat*, March 20, 2015.

Keller, Tim. "The Advent of Humility." *Christianity Today*(2008): 50-53.

King Jr, Martin Luther. "Keep moving from this mountain." *Address at
    Spelman College*, 1960.

Kroll, Luisa & Dolan, Kerry A., "Billionaires: The Richest People
    in the World," *Forbes*, March 5, 2019, www.forbes.com/
    billionaires/#37a67b3251c7.

Lewis, Clive Staples. *Mere Christianity*. Zondervan, 2001.

Luckerson, Victor, "These Are The 10 Most Popular Tweets of All Time," *Time*, March 21, 2016, time.com/4263227/most-popular-tweets/.

March, James G. *Primer on decision making: How decisions happen.* Simon and Schuster, 1994.

Merriam-Webster, s.v. "capitalism," accessed December 10, 2019, https://www.merriam-webster.com/dictionary/capitalism.

Pink, Daniel H. *To sell is human: The surprising truth about moving others.* Penguin, 2013.

Piper, John. "Hope as the motivation of love: 1 Peter 3: 9–12." *New Testament Studies* 26, no. 2 (1980): 212-230.

Plantinga, Alvin. *Warranted Christian Belief.* Oxford University Press on Demand, 2000.

Ruelle, Peter, "Advance in high-pressure physics," *The Harvard Gazette*, January 26, 2017, news.harvard.edu/gazette/story/2017/01/a-breakthrough-in-high-pressure-physics/.

Saiidi, Uptin. "Millennials are Prioritizing Experiences Over Stuff." *CNBC*, May 5, 2016, www.cnbc.com/2016/05/05millenials-are-prioritizing-experiences-over-stuff.html (accessed December 17, 2019).

Schulaka, Carly. "Dan Pink on Why It's OK to Be in Sales, the Importance of Clarity, and a New Way to Innovate." *Journal of Financial Planning* 26, no. 9 (2013): 14.

Schwartz, Barry. *Why we work.* Simon and Schuster, 2015.

Sherry, Suzanna. "Lee v Weisman: Paradox Redux." *The Supreme Court Review* 1992 (1992): 123-153.

Smith, Larry, "Why You Will Fail to Have a Great Career," TedxUW, November 2011.

Stevenson, Bryan. *Just mercy: A story of justice and redemption*. Spiegel & Grau, 2019.

Stevenson Bryan, "We Need to Talk About Injustice," June 8, 2016, https://www.youtube.com/watch?v=c2tOp7OxyQ8 (accessed December 17, 2019).

Wallace, David Foster, "This is Water" Kenyon College Archive, speech, Gambier, Ohio, May 21, 2005, http://bulletin-archive.kenyon.edu/x4280.html (accessed December 17, 2019).

Warren Buffet Archive, "Morning Session—2014 Meeting, May 3, 2014 https://buffett.cnbc.com/video/2014/05/03/morning-session---2014-berkshire-hathaway-annual-meeting.html (accessed December 17, 2019).

Warren, Rick. *The purpose driven life: What on earth am I here for?*. Zondervan, 2012.

White, Jack E., "Martin Luther King," *Time*, April 13, 1998, accessed December 17, 2019 at http://content.time.com/time/magazine/article/0,9171,988163-2,00.html